Anne Steele
and Her Spiritual Vision

Anne Steele
and Her Spiritual Vision:

Seeing God in the Peaks, Valleys,
and Plateaus of Life

Priscilla Wong

Reformation Heritage Books
Grand Rapids, Michigan

Reformation Heritage Books
2965 Leonard St. NE
Grand Rapids, MI 49525
616-977-0889 / Fax 616-285-3246
orders@heritagebooks.org
www.heritagebooks.org

Printed in the United States of America
12 13 14 15 16 17/10 9 8 7 6 5 4 3 2 1

Library of Congress Cataloging-in-Publication Data

Wong, Priscilla.
   Anne Steele and her spiritual vision : seeing God in the peaks, valleys, and plateaus of life / Priscilla Wong.
      p. cm.
   Includes bibliographical references (p.   ).
   ISBN 978-1-60178-185-7 (pbk. : alk. paper) 1. Steele, Anne, 1717-1778. 2. Baptists—England—Biography. 3. Hymn writers—England—Biography. 4. Baptists—Hymns—History and criticism. I. Title.
   BV330.S74W66 2012
   286'.1092—dc23
   [B]
                                        2012027489

For additional Reformed literature, request a free book list from Reformation Heritage Books at the above regular or e-mail address.

Contents

Foreword. vii
Acknowledgments. ix

1. Introduction: Seeing God in the Circumstances of Life 1
2. The Glory of God in Creation. 11
3. Faith in the Face of Suffering 51
4. Hope in the Promised Glory. 91
5. Anne Steele's Hymnody:
    A Window into the Christian Journey. 133

Selected Bibliography 143

Foreword

Even though Anne Steele was the most significant Baptist hymn writer and poetess of the "long" eighteenth century, by the close of the twentieth century her memory was buried under decades of near total oblivion. Thankfully, this has begun to change. In the past few years two major studies of Steele have appeared: John R. Broome's biography of Anne Steele, the first complete life of the poetess, came out in 2007; and then a year later Cynthia Aalders's *To Express the Ineffable*, a study of the theology and artistry of Steele's hymnody, was published. In addition, Julia Griffin has quite recently provided scholars with an erudite and critical edition of the entire Steele corpus, included in the eight-volume series *Nonconformist Women Writers, 1720–1840* (2011), edited by Timothy Whelan. Now, three studies—nay, four if we count this monograph of Priscilla Wong—do not a scholarly trend make. But these studies reveal a serious lacuna in many studies of the eighteenth-century Particular Baptist community: namely, the failure to appreciate certain key roles played by female Baptists such as Steele or her contemporary Anne Dutton, for example, in this era.

Through the medium of the main hymnal of the transatlantic Baptist community, namely, that of John Rippon, Steele's hymns played an especially significant role in shaping the prayers and thoughts of the numerous Baptists who sang them. These hymns were also a factor in the profound renewal and expansion that came to Baptist circles in this period. And so Priscilla Wong's new study of spiritual themes in Anne Steele's hymns is indeed welcome. May it be a means of deepening our appreciation and understanding of Baptist piety in the late eighteenth century, one of the most important eras in the history of God's people.

—Michael A. G. Haykin

Acknowledgments

Anne Steele's hymns and poems would not have been published had it not been for those who facilitated the process of their publication. Devout and gifted pastors and writers encouraged and gave advice to Anne Steele, and her family, having the financial means to do so, bore the cost of publication. Anne Steele's abilities as a writer were thus nurtured by the faith that her friends and family had in her work and her success by their bold and loving insistence that it ought to be surrendered to the public eye. In the same vein, I am deeply indebted to many for the materialization of this book.

This study began as a dissertation that was submitted in fulfillment of the requirements for the master of theological studies degree at Toronto Baptist Seminary (TBS). This book would not have been possible without the help of Dr. Michael Haykin of Southern Baptist Theological Seminary. When I consulted him for topics for my paper, he suggested the piety of Anne Steele as reflected in her hymnody. Furthermore, I would like to express my deep appreciation for his lectures in church history and spirituality, which I had the privilege of listening to during my study at TBS, for they truly opened my eyes to the vast and rich treasures of my Christian heritage and sparked a genuine interest to find out more. It was these lectures that provided me with the necessary background to do further independent research, which ultimately brought this dissertation to fruition.

I am also thankful to Dr. Dennis Ngien of Tyndale Seminary for his continual encouragement over the past several years. It was the recognition received from his Centre for Mentorship and Theological

Reflection that instigated my studies in seminary. I have come to see the value of having a spiritual advisor holding me accountable for what I have been given and directing me toward how to use it.

I would also like to thank Dr. Glendon G. Thompson of Toronto Baptist Seminary for calling me into his office after class one day and advising me to keep on writing. Encounters such as these certainly help to strengthen the resolve of the aspiring writer.

Much thanks, of course, goes to Reformation Heritage Books for agreeing to publish this book and to the RHB staff for all their hard work in preparing this book for publication.

I express grateful appreciation for the extensive work done on Anne Steele by J. R. Broome, Cynthia Y. Aalders, and Sharon James. Their research provided the resources that made it possible for me to focus on key areas of Anne Steele's life and works. Just as they were motivated to contribute to this topic that has received little attention until recent years, I felt compelled to make the life of Anne Steele and her hymns more accessible to today's audience.

Thanks to Jon Oakley for graciously providing me with beautiful photos of Broughton (Steele's hometown), one of which has been used for this book cover.

Thanks to my sister Grace, mother of four, who managed to squeeze in time in her busy schedule to come up with a cover design for this book.

I would also like to show my gratitude to all my family and friends for their continual support of my writing endeavors.

A hearty thanks also to my children—four-year-old Nathaniel and two-year-old Jenuine—for their long afternoon naps afforded me the hours I needed daily to do my writing.

Finally, I owe my deepest gratitude to my husband, Lee—for the many, many sacrifices he made so that I could spend my time studying, researching, and writing; for his relentless support of my writing ambitions; and for his words of encouragement during times when I needed to hear them most.

To God alone be the glory!

*Teach me to begin
the work of heaven below.*

CHAPTER ONE

Introduction: Seeing God in the Circumstances of Life

Only recently has substantial work been done on Anne Steele (1717–1778). Steele was an eighteenth-century British writer of hymns, psalms, poetry, and prose. She has been recognized as one of the leading female hymn writers of her time. In the first extensive biography on Steele, J. R. Broome writes that she "found herself among giants in hymnology and it is important to understand where she is to be placed in that hierarchy of gifted men, for she was in fact the only woman of that period whose hymns have stood the test of time."[1] This is a telling statement of Steele's aptitude for writing, for the "giants" of her time included Isaac Watts (1674–1748), often known as the father of the English hymn; Charles Wesley (1707–1788); Philip Doddridge (1702–1751); John Newton (1725–1807); and William Cowper (1731–1800).

While Steele originally wrote for personal devotional reflection, her father, William Steele, eventually used her hymns for worship services at the Broughton church where he pastored. Steele went on to produce hymns adapted for specific occasions for her church, such as baptism and the Lord's Supper.[2] In 1769 the first hymnbook to include her published hymns was John Ash's and

---

1. J. R. Broome, *A Bruised Reed: The Life and Times of Anne Steele* (Harpenden, U.K.: Gospel Standard Trust Publications, 2007), 151.
2. "Anne Steele regularly composed hymns for services at the chapel, which must have been read, verse by verse, probably by her father from the pulpit, and led by a group of singers with their manuscript tunebooks." Broome, *Bruised Reed*, 214.

Caleb Evans's *A Collection of Hymns Adapted to Public Worship* (known as the Bristol Collection), a book commonly used by Calvinistic Baptists (or Particular Baptists). Of the 412 hymns found in this collection, sixty-two belonged to Steele. A hymnbook that became even more popular was John Rippon's *A Selection of Hymns from the Best Authors,* published in 1787, which included hymns by authors of different denominations. Of its 588 hymns, fifty-three belonged to Steele.[3] According to Rippon, in compiling the collection he sought to "walk abroad and gather up the Golden Ears which have long lain scattered in the Fields of Piety and Genius."[4] The minister had sifted through ninety volumes of hymnbooks, hymns, and psalms in England and America, so it is amazing to consider that from thousands of hymns Steele's represent almost 10 percent of the collection.[5]

---

3. See Cynthia Y. Aalders, *To Express the Ineffable: The Hymns and Spirituality of Anne Steele*, Studies in Baptist History and Thought (Milton Keynes, U.K.: Paternoster, 2008), 40:60–65 for a background of these hymnbooks. See also Broome, *Bruised Reed*, 152.

Fifteen thousand copies of Rippon's hymnbook were sold in Britain within five years of its first publication, and by 1828, two hundred thousand copies had been sold in Britain and one hundred thousand in North America. Ken R. Manley, "'Sing Side by Side': John Rippon and Baptist Hymnody," in *Pilgrim Pathways: Essays in Baptist History in Honour of B. R. White*, ed. William H. Brackney, Paul S. Fiddes, and John H. Y. Briggs (Macon, Ga.: Mercer University Press, 1999), 149, 151.

4. John Rippon, *Selection* (1787), viii, quoted in Manley, "'Sing Side by Side,'" 131.

5. John Rippon (1751–1836), a leading English Baptist minister, felt a need for a collection of hymns (one reason the Bristol Collection became inadequate was that specific subjects and doctrines were not addressed). Theological accuracy was the minister's primary concern: the collection comprised a "distinctly orthodox Calvinist theology" and "a strong evangelistic spirit." Manley, "'Sing Side by Side,'" 130–32, 138, 154.

The only authors in these hymnbooks appearing more than Steele are Watts and Doddridge. Rippon included 101 of Doddridge's hymns and thirty-nine of Watts's (since *Selection* was intended to supplement Watts's own collection, *Hymns and Psalms*). One reason Watts was the Baptists' favorite was because his hymns were "doctrinally orthodox, objective in tone, and

Steele wrote 144 hymns, set thirty-four psalms to verse, and composed numerous poems and prose meditations. The first publication was in 1760, when two volumes of her hymns and poems were published under the title *Poems on Subjects Chiefly Devotional* (her works were published under the pseudonym "Theodosia"). In 1780 a new edition was published under the title *Miscellaneous Pieces in Verse and Prose*, adding a volume of poems and prose reflections. This latter edition opened with a preface on Steele's life by Caleb Evans (1737–1791), a leading London Baptist minister who was also a family friend. It was clear he had deep respect for Steele in the way he wrote of her Christian character:

> The duties of friendship and religion occupied her time, and the pleasures of both constituted her delight. Her heart was "apt to feel" too often to a degree too painful for her own felicity, but always with the most tender and generous sympathies for her friends.... Her life was a life of unaffected humility, warm benevolence, sincere friendship and genuine devotion. A life, which it is not easy truly to describe, or faithfully to imitate.[6]

In 1808, Steele's three volumes of writings were released as a two-volume set in North America under the title *The Works of Miss Anne Steele*. In 1863, another edition was published in London under the title *Hymns, Psalms, and Poems* and included a memoir by John Sheppard in which he expressed his appreciation for Steele:

> Her usefulness has far distanced her fame: she exerts an influence where her history is unknown; she ministers by many a sick bed; she furnishes the song in many a night of affliction. Every Sunday hears her hymns in many churches.... Men use her hymns who never heard her name, and many a one has

---

free from frivolities." Aalders notes that Wesley's perceptible absence from this list was "a matter of theological fidelity": Wesley's theology was Arminian while the Baptists were Calvinistic. Manley, "'Sing Side by Side,'" 130, 132–33; Aalders, *To Express the Ineffable*, 60.

6. As quoted in preface to *Bruised Reed*, by Broome, n.p.

uttered his penitence and desires, in language whose author he never knew.[7]

The most recent edition is a compilation of all of Steele's hymns, published in 1967, which includes a biographical sketch of Steele's life and family history by J. R. Broome.

Steele's life demonstrates remarkable piety and a profound understanding of the workings of God. Her medium of expression was writing, from which the modern reader can draw inspiration and valuable lessons for godly living. D. Bruce Hindmarsh, writing on the value of recovering church history for the purpose of renewing the spirituality of Christians today, says of Steele's hymns, "[Her] religious verse poignantly expresses trust in Christ in the midst of all life's hardships. Her verse is a treasure from the evangelical attic well worth bringing back downstairs."[8] Broome remarks, "While no written record survives of her spiritual experience, yet in her open frank way she reveals much of it indirectly in her hymns, which gives to them a peculiar relevance to succeeding generations of Christians who walk in the same spiritual paths as she did."[9]

Recent Works on Anne Steele

J. R. Broome's biography, *A Bruised Reed: The Life and Times of Anne Steele*, is an exhaustive work, complete with family trees, illustrations of the local landscape, extracts from prefaces appearing in her published works, a thorough account of the historical context (particularly the situation in which Steele's family found themselves as Dissenters of the Calvinistic Baptist denomination, which will be discussed in chapter 3), and an in-depth description of Steele's personal, family, and church life. Broome also examines Steele's

---

7. As quoted in preface to *Bruised Reed*, by Broome, n.p.

8. D. Bruce Hindmarsh, "Retrieval and Renewal: A Model for Evangelical Spiritual Vitality," in *J. I. Packer and the Evangelical Future: The Impact of His Life and Thought*, ed. Timothy George (Grand Rapids: Baker Academic, 2009), 111.

9. Broome, *Bruised Reed,* 173.

writings and, at times, gives the context in which they were written, allowing the reader to see how she responded to particular events and circumstances in her life in light of her Christian faith.[10] Steele's hymns, psalms set to verse, and prose are also included in the book.

Sharon James's book *In Trouble and in Joy: Four Women Who Lived for God* offers a thematic approach to Steele's life and writings, chronicling her life as it reveals how an individual was able to find contentment and joy even in the midst of suffering.[11] James's book is a practical resource for the mainstream reader desiring to become familiar with Steele. The book sheds light on the difficult circumstances Steele faced—as a child of Dissenters, as a woman in the eighteenth century who was not only a writer but willfully single and whose ill health caused her severe pain and discomfort in an age with no anesthetics or benefits of advanced medicine. Although James does not offer a close analysis of Steele's hymns, she provides samples of her work that fall under particular themes.[12] James's book is a good starting point for Broome's considerable one.

---

10. Many spiritual themes found in Steele's hymnody have been addressed by the authors discussed in this chapter. The hymns mentioned in Broome's book, for instance, deal with national matters, scriptural truths, and beliefs pertaining to the Reformed, Calvinistic tradition. According to Broome, among the subjects that emerge from Steele's hymns include the need to have faith in Jesus as the only source of help, happiness, and hope; the vanity and transience of life compared to the life to come; the longing for divine assurance when facing trials of faith; the yearning for complete submission to the will of God; the hope that comes from heaven in times of suffering; the appreciation of God's creation, and above all, His salvation; the sorrows and sufferings of Christ; the reality of sin in humanity; the Holy Spirit as Comforter; and the power of the preached word in the ministry of the gospel. Doctrinally, her hymns cover the Trinity, incarnation, redemption, and the sufferings and resurrection of Christ.

11. Sharon James, *In Trouble and in Joy: Four Women Who Lived for God* (Darlington, U.K.: Evangelical Press, 2003). James's book looks at the lives and writings of Margaret Baxter (1639–1681), Sarah Edwards (1710–1758), Anne Steele, and Frances Ridley Havergal (1836–1879).

12. James's sampling shows that Steele wrote about topics such as the sense of God's presence in the beauties of nature, gratitude for the goodness of God, the temporary nature of earthly things (and the need for preparing for

Cynthia Y. Aalders's book, *To Express the Ineffable: The Hymns and Spirituality of Anne Steele*, presents another dimension to Steele's life and works. While Broome's book largely focuses on the historical and James's book on the thematic, Aalders's book is wider in scope as she examines Steele's life and writings from a historical, theological, and literary perspective. The biographical sketch of Steele is presented to facilitate the study of the spiritual themes emerging from her hymns. Aalders performs a close analysis of Steele's hymns and looks specifically at the themes of ineffability (the seeming impossibility of using human language to express meaningful truths about God), suffering and the silence of God, and resignation and longing. Moreover, Steele's writing is presented not in isolation but with respect to the context in which she wrote—for instance, eighteenth-century Baptist Calvinism, the start of evangelicalism, early Romanticism, and the Age of Sensibility.

Prior to Broome, James, and Aalders, biographical information on Steele was relatively incomplete and even distorted. Dictionaries and biographical entries, however brief and dated, generally highlight Steele's gifted poetic abilities; her piety (one entry identifies Steele as the "female Poet of the Sanctuary");[13] her physical ailments; an alleged drowning incident involving the man she had been courting;[14] her father, William Steele, Baptist minister

---

eternity), the sovereignty of God and the acceptance of suffering, calm resignation to the providence of God, contemplation of heavenly realities in times of pain and sorrow, and devotion to Christ.

13. Henry S. Burrage, *Baptist Hymn Writers and Their Hymns* (Portland, Maine: Brown Thurston and Company, 1888), 46.

14. Many of these earlier entries describe James Elcombe as being her fiancé who drowned while bathing in the river the day before their wedding. However, the Steele family papers provide no explicit indication that Steele was ever engaged to Elcombe. The inaccurate accounts surrounding Elcombe's drowning "have been made that Steele subsequently led a romantically unfulfilled life and that she had no choice but to accept the lonely and disappointed life of a spinster.... This manipulation of her life by her biographers suggests an outmoded and inaccurate cultural construction of gendered identity. The hidden history reveals that Anne Steele was gregarious and socially popular,

of a church in Broughton, whose death in 1769 was devastating to her; and the solemnity of her final words before her own death in 1778, "I know that my Redeemer liveth." These particular scenes taken from her life have, unfortunately, played a part in forming an impression of Steele as merely a victim of tragedy.[15] Assessing this earlier body of information in light of the Steele family archive, which only recently was made available at the Angus Library at Regent's Park College at Oxford University, J. R. Watson and Nancy Cho write:

> The picture of Anne Steele's life and character handed down to us is in fact a collage constructed from selected fragments of her life. The most heart-rending aspects of her life history, her physical suffering and emotional hardships, have been privileged, cut out, and reshaped into a new, reconstituted whole, a mythologised version of Steele's life moulded for the cultural and ontological needs of her biographers and the audiences they were writing for. At the same time, other aspects of her life have been obscured and forgotten from literary history.[16]

With the more recent publications, then, there is the hope of securing a solid grasp of the context in which Steele wrote so that a more accurate picture can be formed of Anne Steele the person—a faithful woman who committed her life and talents to the purpose of glorifying her Creator.

Worth noting in these earlier entries is the attention paid to the uniqueness of Steele's hymns. While acknowledging her lesser technical skill when compared to the likes of Watts or Wesley, they praise her compositions for their emotional quality and honesty. Her hymns have been described as showing "depth and sincerity

---

but the myth of the suffering tragic spinster and hymn writer has been more potent than the reality." J. R. Watson and Nancy Cho, "Anne Steele's Drowned Fiancé," *British Journal for Eighteenth-Century Studies* 28 (2005): 118, 120. See also discussion in Broome, 101–3; in James, *In Trouble and in Joy*, 127–28; and in Aalders, *To Express the Ineffable*, 8–10.

15. Watson and Cho, "Anne Steele's Drowned Fiancé," 118.
16. Watson and Cho, "Anne Steele's Drowned Fiancé," 118.

of feeling,"[17] "full of genuine Christian feeling," displaying "more elegance than force,"[18] giving us the "Hymn of Introspection and of intense devotion to Christ's person, expressed in fervid terms of heightened emotion…[adding] to English Hymnody the plaintive, sentimental note."[19] Her psalms have been described as comparable to Watts's "in literalness, smoothness, and evangelical power."[20]

Broome observes that Steele's hymns possess a deep, personal dimension. Describing her spiritual state, he writes, "Anne had an educated mind, humbled by grace. Hers was not a natural religion, but a religion of the heart. Her hymns reflected things which she had 'heard, seen with her eyes, looked upon, and her hands had handled of the Word of life' [1 John 1:1]."[21] The subjects Steele wrote on speak intimately to the hearts of Christians because she had a real experience of them. This is why modern readers are still able to connect with the subject matter of Steele's writing—her "hymns contain truth, experience, and worship. They will never grow old while Christians continue to experience the grace of God."[22]

Spiritual Themes Explored in This Book

A perusal of Steele's hymns reveals how plainly and genuinely she saw God, even in circumstances when it may have been difficult to do so. Furthermore, Steele's vision did not merely consist of some vague impression or notion of God, but rather her vision involved

17. Louis Benson, *The English Hymn, Its Development and Use in Worship* (New York: Hodder and Stoughton, 1915), 214, quoted in "Anne Steele's 'Psalm 13': A Hymn to Be Mined," *Perspectives in Religious Studies* 25, no. 1 (1998): 127–28.

18. *The New Schaff-Herzog Encyclopedia of Religious Knowledge*, 4th ed., s.v. "Steele, Anne."

19. Benson, *The English Hymn*, 538.

20. *The Baptist Encyclopedia: A Dictionary of the Doctrines, Ordinances, Usages, Confessions of Faith, Sufferings, Labors, and Successes, and of the General History of the Baptist Denomination in All Lands*, rev. ed., s.v. "Steele, Miss Anna."

21. Broome, *Bruised Reed*, 175.

22. Broome, *Bruised Reed*, 175.

seeing the dynamic and intricate workings of her Creator. By unpacking the spiritual themes of Steele's hymns, then, deep theological truths can be extracted.

This book will examine three themes found in Steele's hymnody, all of which relate to how she was able to see God in different circumstances of her life. First, it will examine the way Steele was able to see God in her everyday living, in the creation that surrounded her. Second, it will look at how Steele was able to see God in her suffering. Third, it will reflect on how Steele was able to maintain a strong vision of heaven even as she resided on earth. These three themes touch upon the various points that are encountered in the Christian journey—in life's seeming ordinariness, in life's inevitable adversity, and in life's perpetual quest for that which lies beyond.

Chapters 2, 3, and 4 will each address the above spiritual themes. Prior to hymn analysis, the chapters will begin with a general explanation of the theology behind the spiritual theme to be explored (set within the framework of John Gill's theological writings, since Steele was familiar with this Baptist theologian's work) and a proper historical context as it pertains to Steele's life.

The objective is that a close analysis of Steele's hymns in relation to specific themes will not only establish a more coherent and intimate picture of her life and spirituality, but also cultivate a more intense desire for Christians to grow in their faith and understanding of God.

Let the sons of science rove
through the boundless fields of space,
and amazing wonders trace;
bright worlds beyond those starry flames,
my nobler curiosity inspire.

CHAPTER TWO

The Glory of God
in Creation

Anne Steele plainly perceived God in creation. British Particular Baptist pastor and theologian John Gill (1697–1771), whose works Steele appreciated, wrote that the chief end of creation is the glory of God (Prov. 16:4; Rom. 1:20; Jer. 32:17).[1] One of Gill's most important works, *A Body of Practical and Doctrinal Divinity*, expounds at length on the subject of creation.[2] God's goodness, power, and majesty are furthermore manifested in His plan of redemption for fallen humanity: "The world and all things were made for the sake of God's chosen people."[3] Creation is therefore the stage on which God's plan of redemption is carried out. Consequently, the impetus for God's people is to glorify Him.[4] Thankfulness and trust are to be rendered to the almighty Creator.

God is not only the author of creation, but also the one who upholds and governs it. Gill likens God not to an architect who builds a house and then takes leave of it, but to the builder who is intimately involved with its structure: "Without his support and government of it, it could not long subsist: besides, there must be some ends for which it is created; which ends it cannot attain and

---

1. John Gill, *A Body of Practical and Doctrinal Divinity*, The Baptist Faith Series (Paris, Ark.: The Baptist Standard Bearer, 2001), 2:181.
2. William Steele Sr. was among the list of subscribers to John Gill's three-volume *Body of Divinity* published in 1769. His will records that his library of books was handed down to his daughter Anne. Broome, *Bruised Reed*, 213.
3. Gill, *Body of Practical and Doctrinal Divinity*, 181.
4. Gill, *Body of Practical and Doctrinal Divinity*, 181.

answer of itself; but must be directed and influenced by the Creator of it."[5] In Paul's address to the Athenians in Acts 17, the apostle explains that people are created by God and exist only as a result of His providence: "God that made the world and all things therein, seeing that he is Lord of heaven and earth…giveth to all life, and breath, and all things…. In him we live, and move, and have our being" (vv. 24–25, 28). God's people therefore ought to recognize that the blessings they experience daily in their lives are evidences of His providential goodness.[6]

The doctrines of creation and providence impart theological truths that are instrumental to understanding God and how He relates to and interacts with the people in this world. Seeing Him as the author of our being, the originator and sustainer of creation, and the planner and revealer of redemption should move us to widen our perspective when it comes to regarding our own role in the world that He created. The ensuing narrative and hymn analyses will demonstrate that Steele possessed such a vision and that much can be observed from her daily encounters and interactions with the world around her.

The Creation Surrounding Anne Steele: Beauties of the Countryside

Steele was deeply conscious of the natural landscape around her, and creation and providence are recurring themes in her writings. Living in the Broughton countryside, with acres of green pastures and hills at her doorstep, Steele was free to explore and enjoy the beauties that saturated the outdoors. The atmosphere suited her temperament. More reserved and timid compared to her half-sister, Mary, Anne was withdrawn in social settings and often longed for home when traveling outside of her hometown.[7] She preferred the

---

5. Gill, *Body of Practical and Doctrinal Divinity*, 193.
6. Gill, *Body of Practical and Doctrinal Divinity*, 194.
7. Marjorie Reeves, *Pursuing the Muses: Female Education and Nonconformist Culture, 1700–1900* (London: Leicester University Press, 1997), 67.

life of tranquility and seclusion over the public one with all of its hectic activity and shallow forms of entertainment.[8]

Steele spent the greater part of her life in this quiet village. The closest urbanized area to Broughton was Salisbury, which was twelve miles away. Her home since childhood was known as "Grandfathers," a house that had been occupied by generations of the Steele family. It was located in the south part of Broughton, along a path of other houses and thatch cottages, and the immediate landscape boasted a river valley, with Hampshire's rolling chalk hills adorning the east and west horizon.[9] Steele's own bedroom had a breathtaking view of the River Wallop, a trout stream that flowed through meadow and woodland before joining its main channel, the River Test.[10] Such were Steele's companions—murmuring waters brimming with aquatic life, wildflowers scattered on lush velvet slopes,

---

8. In a letter written to her half-sister, Mary, Steele writes, "I think I have heretofore found as much pleasure scribbling in my lonely retirement as a fine Lady could do at a Ball, glittering among a crowd of Belles and Beaus. —poor comparison—'Tis true I can have no notion of the high delight those gay flutterers taste, but as I imagine they are generally strangers to serious reflection, I think their entertainments deserve not to be named with the pleasure enjoy'd by a contemplative mind." Sylviana (Anne Steele) to Mary Wakeford (n.d.), STE 3/10 ix, Angus Library, Regent's Park College, Oxford; quoted in James, *In Trouble and in Joy,* 135–36.

In the spring of 1751, Anne and Mary, being ill, stayed in Bath for almost two months hoping to improve their health. In an unpublished poem, Steele expresses her yearning for home: "Dear native rural scenes for you I sigh.... And fly the laughing crowds and gay parade." "On Walks in Bath," Anne Steele, STE 3/3, Angus Library, Regent's Park College, Oxford; quoted in Broome, *Bruised Reed,* 123–24.

Consider also the following account: "Anne Steele, both on account of an accident in girlhood and heavy attacks of illness at not infrequent intervals, loved the retirement of her Hampshire home. A quiet life suited her best. The garish foppery of fashion and the loud-voiced frequenters of life's dusty arena were little suited to her taste." Mrs. E. R. Pitman, *Lady Hymn-Writers* (London, 1892), 69, quoted in J. R. Watson, *The English Hymn: A Critical and Historical Study* (New York: Oxford University Press, 1997), 422.

9. Broome, *Bruised Reed,* 74.

10. Broome, *Bruised Reed,* 169.

and sheep bells tinkling in the distance as the flock ambled across the grassland.

This idyllic setting enabled Steele to reflect on the more profound aspects of life. It is no surprise that she derived much of her poetic inspiration here, and some of her verses were composed in the garden at "Grandfathers."[11] Steele also likely had her own personal retreat, a simple shelter at "Grandfathers," a perfect solitary escape for the introverted writer, offering her an intimate view of the open air. In a letter written to Mary in 1750, Steele describes the enchanting scene by her window: "My cell too has its charms. The honeysuckle at my window is in full bloom and I am sometimes entertained with the soft warbling of a neighbouring nightingale.... The rural scenes are in their perfection."[12]

Steele's father owned farm and timber businesses, and their success brought great security and comfort to the family (the Steeles eventually owned about five hundred acres of farmland). Her father and brother frequently went away to manage the family businesses; meanwhile Steele stayed at home, writing.[13] Even while away, Steele's

---

11. According to Aalders, John Sheppard speculates this in his 1863 memoir of Steele, *Hymns, Psalms, and Poems*. Aalders, *To Express the Ineffable*, 71.

12. Anne Steele to Mary Steele Wakeford (May 7, 1750), STE 3/9/i, Angus Library, Regent's Park College, Oxford; quoted in Broome, *Bruised Reed*, 121.

13. See Broome, *Bruised Reed*, 126, 224, 236. Broome provides a valuable perspective on the family's home life, work ethic, and contribution to the local community: "Anne Steele had lived her life surrounded by a hive of activity. She and her stepmother had both at times complained about the constant activities and travels of William and his father.... Anne had felt that her father and her brother were too deeply involved in their business activities to the detriment of their family life. But the Puritan ethic of work was deeply engrained in the Steele family and from the days of old Henry Steele [Steele's father's uncle], who had founded the timber business and established contracts with the Admiralty and later invested his profits in farming, the family had prospered.... No doubt the village of Broughton had benefited, many of the villagers being employed in the family businesses. Also the Broughton Baptist Church had been liberally provided with funds by the family.... [But] while business was important in the family, the church and spiritual things were their primary concern.... It is a wonder how Henry Steele and William

brother, William, identified with his sister's love of nature. In the summer of 1742, during a business trip to Lewes, William wrote a letter to her describing the scenery there:

> Mr Pope's *Letters* have agreeably entertained me all morn-ing in the garden, which being rising ground, adjoining to a fine valley, enriched by a noble river. [The Ouse] is by nature the finest terrace you can imagine, from whence is a beautiful prospect of the town of Lewes, on an eminence at half-a-mile distance across the valley; an old ruined castle on a high hill almost in the middle of the town which seems with its nod-ding walls to threaten the inhabitants, and the lofty mountains which surround the country give it a very romantic air; it is I think on the whole, though not the most extensive, yet one of the most charming landscapes I have seen.[14]

The rustic beauty of their childhood home nurtured a romantic spirit in both siblings. Growing up, brother and sister, who were only two years apart in age, must have roamed the countryside together on many occasions.[15]

Steele's contentment in her reclusive life and her attachment to her family were likewise evident in her decision to remain single. In 1742, she turned down a marriage proposal from pastor and Bap-tist hymn writer Benjamin Beddome (1717–1795). A letter written to Mary fifteen years later would reveal Steele's perspective on mar-riage as she compared the life of matrimony to a path with "a great many thorns."[16] As Broome observes, "Anne preferred the quiet

---

Steele senior managed their businesses and pastorates at the same time. It is evident that they led highly organized lives and made excellent use of their time." Broome, *Bruised Reed*, 224.

14. Broome, *Bruised Reed*, 110. Steele's writings show that she read the works of the great Enlightenment poet Alexander Pope (1688–1744). A com-monplace book compiled by her brother provides evidence of his reading various works by Pope. For a list of these works, see Broome, *Bruised Reed*, 213–14 and Aalders, *To Express the Ineffable*, 184–85.

15. Broome, *Bruised Reed*, 74.

16. Anne Steele to Mary (n.d.), STE 3/10/xiv, Angus Library, Regent's Park College, Oxford; quoted in Broome, *Bruised Reed*, 112.

life of Broughton, rather than being a pastor's wife among a big congregation and having a large family of children."[17] While Mary expressed a different sentiment (in 1749, she married Joseph Wakeford and moved to Andover), Broome surmises that Steele probably would not have produced as much writing had she chosen to settle down and raise a family.[18]

---

17. Broome, *Bruised Reed*, 112–14. Worth noting are the verses found in Benjamin Beddome's memoir, written in 1742, the year he proposed to Steele, revealing the kind of woman he desired to marry and how he deemed Steele to possess such a character: "Let the companion of my youth/Be one of innocence and truth; /Let modest charms adorn her face, /And give her thy superior grace. /By heavenly art first make her thine, /Then make her willing to be mine." Broome, *Bruised Reed*, 112. See also Michael A. G. Haykin, "Benjamin Beddome and Anne Steele," in *The Christian Lover: The Sweetness of Love and Marriage in the Letters of Believers* (Lake Mary, Fla.: Reformation Trust, 2009), 31–35.

18. For extracts of the correspondence between Anne and Mary on the subject of marriage and singleness, see James, *In Trouble and in Joy*, 156–61. Reeves calls attention to the series of letters written between Steele and Mary in the 1750s (after Mary is married) that "highlights the struggle of a wife and mother to concentrate on serious reflections and writing." Mary bore three children: William in 1753, Samuel in 1754, and Mary in 1760. In 1769, Mary writes a light-hearted poem to Polly (Anne's brother's daughter, whose real name was Mary) on the "intellectual constraints of married life," disclosing her "realization that marriage has shut the door on her pursuit of the Muses." Reeves, *Pursuing the Muses*, 88–92.

While Steele chose not to marry, she nonetheless saw marriage as a blessing for those who chose that path. On several occasions, she wrote poems in honor of the nuptials of those close to her. In an unpublished poem she writes, "May blooming health and calm content be yours, /and love and friendship blend their sweetest charms/to soften care." "A Friend on His Marriage," Anne Steele (October 6, 1743), STE 3/3, Angus Library, Regent's Park College, Oxford; quoted in Broome, *Bruised Reed*, 114.

Although Steele never became a mother, she served as mentor/guardian to several of the younger generation in her family. Jane and Caroline Attwater, Steele's second cousins, were close companions to Steele (we will learn more in chapter 4 of Steele's influence on Jane Attwater). Polly came to rely on Steele as a mother figure upon her mother's death in 1762 when Polly was only nine years old. Steele educated Polly between the ages of eight and fourteen, and cared for her until her brother remarried in 1768. After Steele's death in

But the beauty and tranquility of country life were not the only matters that occupied Steele's mind. Her contemplative nature was rooted in her keen awareness of the divine hand in it all, and hence its temporality:

> Surrounding her were all the signs of the transience of life, as the mortality rate among babies and children was very high, epidemics of smallpox and tuberculosis broke out and her own health was constantly in a precarious state. While she appreciated the hand of God in creation, much more she appreciated His hand in salvation, and this occupied her thoughts far more than her surroundings.[19]

While in her writings Steele celebrated the beauty of nature, she meditated equally on its transience. Marjorie Reeves observes in Steele's poetry that "meditation is often linked with both the beauties and

---

1778, Polly wrote of her aunt, "Where that maternal friend, whose watchful care, /whose fond, assiduous tenderness sustained/my helpless childhood?" See Broome, *Bruised Reed*, 178–79, 186–87, 218.

In 1763, Steele wrote a letter to her brother that included a postscript to Polly, which shows the kind of spiritual figure she was to the younger ones: "O that your mind may be early improved by divine Grace with a sense of your need of this almighty Saviour and that you may be enabled to believe in him and obey him…. Don't go to bed one night or come down one morning without praying to God for his Grace. This advice I have given you before, but I fear you do not think of it constantly, and wish that this letter may help you to remember it." Anne Steele to William Steele, from Broughton (January 5, 1763), STE/8, Angus Library, Regent's Park College, Oxford; quoted in James, *In Trouble and in Joy*, 164. Describing Steele's role in these younger ones' lives, Broome writes, "She was a God-fearing, exercised, praying woman, and though having no children of her own, yet she was surrounded with these growing teenagers, who obviously enjoyed her company, loved her and valued her interest and advice, knowing she had their real welfare at heart." Broome, *Bruised Reed*, 188.

Following the footsteps of Watts, who wrote a collection of poems titled *Divine Songs for the Use of Children*, Steele also wrote verses for the children in her family. The collection of poems was published after her death in 1788, and in 1806 were titled *Verses for Children*. Broome remarks, "The conversion of the young was something that was never forgotten by the Nonconformists." Broome, *Bruised Reed*, 180–82.

19. Broome, *Bruised Reed*, 169.

the changes of the natural world."[20] In Steele's poem "An Evening Walk," meditation is the "pleasing guest" that enables her to "trace the beauties of the vernal scene." Yet in the next line Steele writes, "Beauties, ah how short their boast!...Melancholy thought—away." The magnificence of creation served as a reminder to Steele of what was of eternal value.

Influences of the Pre-Romantic Era:
An Affinity to the Beauty of Nature

Steele's rural background and introspective disposition corresponded perfectly to the ideals characteristic of the Romantic age. James notes that during this period, "many found solace in contemplation of the beauties of nature. It became popular to repudiate the mannered and artificial, in favour of the natural and spontaneous. Rural life was praised; there was a retreat into sentiment and 'sensibility.'"[21] The distinguishing qualities of Romanticism no doubt influenced Steele, considering many of her hymns and poems were reflections on the beauties of nature.

Although the Romantic era primarily refers to the first four decades of the nineteenth century, it can be traced back to the previous century to include Pre-Romantics.[22] The Pre-Romantic era was a rather ambivalent period, as the latter half of the eighteenth century in England saw concomitant ideals of the Classical (or Age of Enlightenment) and Romantic—the former exhibiting "rational order and symmetry," and the latter "spontaneity, fragmentation, and organicism."[23] A major aspect of Pre-Romanticism was what

---

20. Reeves, *Pursuing the Muses,* 77–79.

21. James, *In Trouble and in Joy,* 119–20.

22. Bernard M. G. Reardon, *Religion in the Age of Romanticism: Studies in Early Nineteenth-Century Thought* (New York: Cambridge University Press, 1985), 2.

23. Inger S. B. Brodey, "On Pre-Romanticism or Sensibility: Defining Ambivalences," in *A Companion to European Romanticism,* ed. Michael Ferber (Malden, Mass.: Blackwell Publishing, 2005), 10. Brodey explains the basis for the emergence of the term "Pre-Romantic": "English letters has had no 'Storm and Stress' period, no established name to give to a long transition

was called "Sensibility."[24] Associated with this term were any of the following ideas:

> Ethical thought that stressed the significance of feeling over reason for moral behaviour, resulting in a new psychology that stressed the ethical, didactic, and emotional effect of the faculty of sight…. A consistent preference for rural simplicity over urbanity…. A deep ambivalence about the desirability of order and system.[25]

Sensibility therefore saw feeling as the "supreme human faculty" rather than reason.[26] There was an increased perceptibility and emotional sensitivity that was stimulated by beauty or suffering.[27] For instance, sensibility "brought with it an emphasis on receptivity or sensitivity to external behaviour and sights, whether the landscape garden, the Alps, or the sight of human suffering at home…. [There was] a growing emphasis on nature, natural simplicity, the ordinary, everyday rustic life, and also kindness to animals."[28]

The above explanation of Pre-Romanticism appears to support Aalders's view of Steele's writing, which she observes did not strictly reflect the qualities of a specific period but rather exhibited

---

between periods that appear so different in nature. As a result, there has been a tendency for Romanticism—already so voluminous and variable that the term can hardly bear its own weight—to swallow half of the eighteenth century as well, through the term 'Pre-Romantic,' a term that stems from observations made in the 1930s of conspicuous parallels between European music and literature of the 1740s to the 1790s." Brodey, "On Pre-Romanticism or Sensibility," 10–11.

24. This is a term that Brodey uses instead of Pre-Romanticism since "it treats the literary, aesthetic, and philosophical developments as important in their own right rather than as premonition of future developments." Rather than claiming that Sensibility is a unique period, the term is used to provide a more suitable way of recognizing the set of transitions appearing in the latter half of the eighteenth century in Britain. Brodey, "On Pre-Romanticism or Sensibility," 12.

25. Brodey, "On Pre-Romanticism or Sensibility," 14.

26. Brodey, "On Pre-Romanticism or Sensibility," 14.

27. Brodey, "On Pre-Romanticism or Sensibility," 18.

28. Brodey, "On Pre-Romanticism or Sensibility," 18–19.

qualities associated with different periods. She asserts that multiple historical contexts influenced Steele's writing, including the Age of Enlightenment,[29] the Age of Sensibility,[30] and the Age of Pre-Romanticism and Romanticism.[31]

The suggestion that Steele's writing would have reflected different periods is indeed plausible. In Bernard M. G. Reardon's attempt to define both Classicism and Romanticism, he states that "it may well be that classical and romantic are not mutually exclusive; that classical art has not seldom exhibited a romantic vein, and that romantic art by no means repudiates the virtues we are wont to think of as classical.... 'Classical' and 'romantic' are simply convenient labels to apply to differing outlooks and attitudes of mind that coexist in all ages and frequently in the same individual."[32]

---

29. Linked to the Age of Enlightenment, for instance, were the eighteenth-century ideals of rationalism, confidence, and order. Artistically, this classical style translated to a smooth and perfect form. For Steele, specifically, the Classical style was made evident in her writing by her "clarity of expression, didacticism, and formal, refined qualities." Aalders, *To Express the Ineffable*, 90. The frequent usage of the rhymed couplet in Steele's hymns, for example, demonstrates the polished and instructive nature of her verse, features of Classicism. Aalders, *To Express the Ineffable*, 89.

30. Falling between the Age of the Enlightenment and the Age of Romanticism was the Age of Sensibility (Aalders dates this period between 1740 and 1780, which is also the time during which Steele did much of her writing). The Age of Sensibility was marked by a keenness for morality, aestheticism, introspection, and sentimentalism. Aalders, *To Express the Ineffable*, 118–19. Steele's writing exhibited qualities of the Age of Sensibility in her expression of intense emotion, particularly when it came to the subject of suffering. Aalders, *To Express the Ineffable*, 119. Consequently, while her poetic form was clean and precise, as the Classical style would have demanded, the content was not necessarily so.

31. Aalders observes that it is the particular themes found in Steele's hymns that reflect the Age of Pre-Romanticism or Romanticism. For example, such themes include the yearning for and contemplation of the infinite (i.e., the desire to be in God's presence) and the beauties of nature. Aalders, *To Express the Ineffable*, 156.

32. Reardon, *Religion in the Age of Romanticism*, 1–2. At the same time, classifying Steele's writing according to specific periods must not be given

At the same time, many Romantics of the eighteenth century adopted a pantheistic perspective of creation, deifying the beauties of nature, seeing God *in* nature itself. But Steele saw the whole realm of creation as coming *under* the order and control of God. On the one hand, the Enlightenment centered on the mind and reason; on the other hand, Romanticism on the heart and feelings.[33] Steele's

---

more attention than is constructive to the discussion of the spiritual themes found in her hymns. A writer can be "more concerned with the needs of the text as an internally consistent object than as a vehicle for the promotion of certain historically determined views and values." Lee Patterson, in his essay "Literary History," continues by arguing that there is an "inherent ahistoricity of literary writing," and "any attempt to locate literature within the causal processes of historical explanation must fail. Since historical documents are inextricably dependent upon the events of their historical moment, they can be accounted for by the same covering laws that govern historical explanation per se. But literature evades explanation entirely. On the contrary, it both signifies in ways unique to itself and refers not to merely local historical process but to transhistorical values implicit within the human condition as a whole." Lee Patterson, "Literary History," in *Critical Terms for Literary Study*, ed. Frank Lentricchia and Thomas McLaughlin (Chicago: University of Chicago Press, 1995), 254.

33. David Calhoun, "The Great Divide: Enlightenment and Romanticism," Covenant Theological Seminary, St. Louis, Missouri, spring 2006, accessed May 28, 2011, http://worldwidefreeresources.com/upload/CH320_T_22.pdf. Calhoun provides a valuable perspective on the influence of the Enlightenment and Romanticism on church history as well as their relationship to the Christian faith. He writes: "If the Enlightenment leads in a Deistic direction, to a distant creator God, the great geometrician, Pantheism is the direction of Romanticism.... Since the eighteenth century, Western man and woman have an Enlightenment mind and a Romantic heart till we are brought under the control of Jesus Christ so that our minds and our hearts are now given to Him. We have this split personality with an Enlightenment mind and a Romantic heart. The Enlightenment mind means that people believe that we can solve problems. We can find an answer eventually to everything. Problems are there to be solved. And we have succeeded in solving so many of them that at least for a while there was a hope that we could solve all of them.... The Romantics taught us, while we are solving problems and thinking great rational thoughts, to live life according to our feelings, our desires, what we want to do.... But if the Enlightenment has solved some very big problems, it has not solved the biggest problems. They are still with us. And the Romantic heart has proven

mind and heart, however, were centered on Jesus Christ.[34] Indeed Steele was an intellectual, though she lived in an era that offered limited education to women.[35] Her writings demonstrate that she

---

to be what Isaiah calls 'the deluded heart' as people realize sooner or later that to obey yourself is not a good idea."

34. Broome writes of Steele's hymns, "She is at her best when writing on the sufferings of Christ," while Aalders writes, "Steele's faith, and the expression of that faith in her hymnody, cannot be appreciated completely without some consideration given to her powerful devotion to the person of Christ." Broome, *Bruised Reed*, 175, and Aalders, *To Express the Ineffable*, 168.

35. "A great deal of the education on offer in the early and middle decades of the eighteenth century must have been woefully inadequate for young women hungry for real learning." Reeves later describes Steele's dissatisfaction with the education made available to her. She notes that Steele's "mental and spiritual growth must be attributed mainly to her father and to the wide circle of friends that the Steeles attracted." Her father may have encouraged them to be "bolder and more inquisitive in their reading." The Steeles's circle of friends included John Lavington (c. 1690–1759), Philip Furneaux (1726–1783), James Fanch (1704–1767), Caleb Evans, and John Ash (1724–1779). Such influential figures must have engaged in theological as well as literary discussions with the family. Later in Steele's life, there is seen to be a connection between her family and Mary Scott (poet) as well as Hannah More (poet, playwright, and writer). Reeves, *Pursuing the Muses*, 18, 26–28.

Broome writes that Steele's "abilities, which brought the family into prominence in the eighteenth century through her published works...gave credence to the view that there was much latent ability among women that could be developed with better education." Broome, *Bruised Reed*, 212–13.

Broome cites a diary entry by Steele's stepmother showing that she recognized Steele's talent: "My desires being drawn out concerning the children going to a school, desiring it may be prevented if the Lord saw it best, yet I have often thought the providence of God did direct it.... I now think, as I have before, whether God has not designed some work for this, His young servant...though [Mrs. Steele] could not have realised that her [stepdaughter's] poetry and hymns would still be in print and in use in the twenty-first century." Diaries of Anne [Cator] Steele, vol. 2 (April 2, 1733), STE 2/1/1, Angus Library, Regent's Park College, Oxford; quoted in Broome, *Bruised Reed*, 84.

According to Broome, the quality of writing in William Steele Sr.'s letters reveal that he was an educated man, and that his background influenced the kind of education he wanted for his children: "There is no doubt that, in the Nonconformist academies there was a much broader range of subjects studied, not limited as at Oxford and Cambridge to a strong emphasis on classical

read widely[36] and that she possessed a high regard for the quest for knowledge.[37] Yet in her poem "On Reason," Steele recognized that even reason itself comes from God:

> Reason, the glory of the human frame,
> Eye of the mind, the stamp of heav'n impress'd
> On man alone, of all the various ranks
> Of being, which the great Creator form'd,
> To people numberless this earthly globe,
> *To man alone he gave this ray divine,*
> *This emanation of the deity.*[38]

---

studies and mathematics, but embracing literature, history, modern and classical languages, geography, natural philosophy, logic, elocution and astronomy. It would seem highly likely that William Steele's outlook was shaped in such an academy and that contact with this influence affected the whole of Anne Steele's life." Broome, *Bruised Reed*, 213. Steele's father also had the financial resources to provide better education for his daughters. Steele had attended a Particular Baptist school at Trowbridge as well as almost half a year in a boarding school. However, after 1733 when Steele was sixteen, she apparently received no further education. Broome, *Bruised Reed*, 68, 69, 85, 213.

36. Steele inherited all of her father's books. For a list of these books, see Broome, *Bruised Reed*, 213. See also Aalders, *To Express the Ineffable*, 183–85, for a list of books Steele read.

37. After Steele's death in 1778, Steele's niece Polly, whom she educated during her early years, wrote of her aunt: "My dearest pleasures, my most loved employments, /she taught me first to relish, first awaked/the wish for knowledge." Anne Steele, *Miscellaneous Pieces in Verse and Prose by Theodosia, Collected Works* (Bristol, U.K.: W. Pine, 1780), 3:xii–xvii; quoted in Broome, *Bruised Reed*, 179. Reeves cites a poem of Steele that shows her concern for Polly's intellectual development, part of which reads, "For reason's empire never knew a slave, /Her sway is gentle and her laws are kind." "Reason's Empire," 1780 edition, 3:87, cited in Reeves, *Pursuing the Muses*, 82.

In the preface of the 1780 edition of Steele's published works, Caleb Evans describes Steele as possessing a "capacious soaring mind." Reeves observes that some of Steele's poems show her "determination to distance herself from the superficial pursuits supposed to characterize female life and instead to cultivate the mind." Reeves, *Pursuing the Muses*, 76.

38. Anne Steele, "On Reason," in *The Works of Mrs. Anne Steele: Complete in Two Volumes. Comprehending Poems on Subjects Chiefly Devotional: and Miscellaneous Pieces in Prose and Verse: Heretofore Published under the Title*

The enlightenment gained from reason, along with the pleasures derived from the beauties of nature, are merely revelations
of the divine: "The human mind, like nature, knows alternate light
and shade."[39] The expression of feelings, the "filling of the senses"
in response to the beauties of nature, in and of itself, is insufficient:

> ...all th' enchanting scene
> Is harmony and beauty: nature's charms
> Subdue the heart, and ev'ry sense is fill'd!
>
> ...Think, wither does the soft enchantment tend?
> Are nature's various beauties lent for this,
> Only to please the sense? For nobler ends
> The God of nature gave them.[40]

Rather the "perfect system" discernible in nature—its remarkable
balance and symmetry translating to harmony and beauty—inspires
grander thoughts and directs the human heart to profounder truth:

> The parts of nature in their just proportion,
> Uniting, harmonizing, blend to form
> One perfect system; truth and beauty smile,
> Inviting contemplation upward still.[41]

Steele was able to fully immerse herself in the beauty around her
because she understood its source: "All the enjoyments of nature without the kind influences of [God's] grace are weariness and vanity....
But sweetened with the hope of his favour, and enjoyed as blessings
from the hand of an indulgent Father, every comfort of life acquires a

---

of *Theodosia* (Boston: Munroe, Francis and Parker, 1808), 193–96 (emphasis
mine). Here and throughout this book, the original spelling, capitalization,
and punctuation of Anne Steele's hymns and prose have been retained.

39. Steele, "To Delia," *Poems on Subjects Chiefly Devotional & Miscellaneous Pieces*, 201.

40. Steele, "The Pleasures of Spring," *Poems on Subjects Chiefly Devotional
& Miscellaneous Pieces*, 206.

41. Steele, "The Pleasures of Spring," *Poems on Subjects Chiefly Devotional
& Miscellaneous Pieces*, 207.

power to entertain and please."[42] This divine consciousness is richly expressed in her hymns, as we shall see in the sections to follow.

Creation and Providence in the Hymns of Anne Steele
Theological Insights from "Meditating on Creation and Providence"
The first hymn to be examined is Steele's "Meditating on Creation and Providence."[43] Several key themes associated with these doctrines, which she calls attention to in this hymn, will be considered. In the subsequent sections of this chapter, similar hymns by Steele will be examined to see how she expresses or elaborates on these themes. This will serve to uncover ideas central to Steele's understanding of the doctrines of creation and providence.

The first verse of the hymn highlights the important duty of meditating on God's creation. Upon doing so, the speaker,[44] the watchful observer, is directed to the divine Creator.

> Lord, when my raptur'd thought surveys
> Creation's beauties o'er,

---

42. Steele, *Miscellaneous Pieces in Verse and Prose by Theodosia*, included in Broome, *Bruised Reed*, 344.

43. Steele, Hymn 3, *Poems on Subjects Chiefly Devotional & Miscellaneous Pieces*, 27–29. In this 1808 edition of Steele's manuscript, the hymns are not numbered. In the 1967 edition, the hymns are numbered. The hymn ordering for both editions are the same. As such, both the hymn title and hymn number have been provided for the reader's reference.

44. Throughout this book, the term "speaker" will be used to distinguish between the hymn's author and its speaker. This distinction takes into consideration the gap between the deceased author who penned the hymn and the "imaginary voice" that is experienced by the singer/reader at hand. One of the reasons is that the hymn is not simply the record of an event that once took place, but produces the effect of a "speech event" whenever it is sung/read: "Our experience of hearing (or overhearing) a voice in this text, then, is an illusion created by ourselves because of the way we have been trained to read all writing as if it were speech. Rather than hearing voices from beyond the grave, we create those voices ourselves through an interpretative interaction with written words on a page." See Michael Bath and Tom Furniss, "Hearing Voices in Poetic Texts," in *Reading Poetry: An Introduction* (Hertfordshire: Prentice Hall, 1996), 159–61.

> All nature joins to teach thy praise,
>   And bid my soul adore.

God does not leave this observer in obscurity but leaves behind resounding evidence of His presence. Consider the two commanding images in verse 2 below, "radiant footsteps" and "ten thousand pleasing wonders": the former image invites the observer to follow in its path; the latter presents the majesty of *all* creation ascending and paying tribute to the almighty Creator, which is all the more enticing to the observer.

> Where'er I turn my gazing eyes,
>   Thy radiant footsteps shine;
> Ten thousand pleasing wonders rise,
>   And speak their source divine.

Both of the above verses use words that clarify what is required for fruitful observation: the speaker's thought *surveys* creation, the speaker's eyes are *gazing*; the act of observing is not narrow but wide, not momentary but lingering.

Opening her eyes and meditating on creation, the speaker encounters God's revelation. The subsequent verses make known the vastness and profundity of what lies before her. Verses 3 to 8 shine the spotlight on different aspects of creation and identify their splendor. Verses 3 and 4, for instance, point out the innumerable forms of living creatures that occupy the "earth, and sea, and air." All of these creatures, the conspicuous ones and the subtlest of them (those likely to escape the cursory glance), depend on God's provision for their survival.

> The living tribes of countless forms,
>   In earth, and sea, and air;
> The meanest flies, the smallest worms,
>   Almighty pow'r declare.
>
> All rose to life at thy command,
>   And wait their daily food
> From thy paternal, bounteous hand,
>   Exhaustless spring of good!

Moving across the natural landscape, verse 5 depicts the bright colors of lush green meadows and golden cornfields, which, by God's hand, flourish; verse 6, the growth and diversity of trees and flowers, whose God-endowed beauty affirm their Creator's goodness; verse 7, the revitalizing sun and rain, vehicles of God used to nourish the earth; and verse 8, the radiant moon and stars, over whose sheer brightness even the blackest night cannot prevail.

> The meads, array'd in smiling green,
>   With wholesome herbage crown'd;
> The fields with corn, a richer scene,
>   Spread thy full bounties round.

> The fruitful tree, the blooming flow'r,
>   In varied charms appear;
> Their varied charms display thy pow'r,
>   Thy goodness all declare.

> The sun's productive quick'ning beams
>   The growing verdure spread;
> Refreshing rains and cooling streams
>   His gentle influence aid.

> The moon and stars his absent light
>   Supply with borrow'd rays,
> And deck the sable[45] veil of night,
>   And speak their Maker's praise.

Following this dramatic presentation of the landscape, Steele proceeds with theological reflection, which, according to Watson, is a technique characteristic of Steele's hymns.[46] The final six verses illustrate essential theological truths about creation.

First, the crown of creation is man. Yet, like all other creation, his very breath is maintained by God. Man owes God his utmost

---

45. "Black, dark." Samuel Johnson, *Dictionary of the English Language* (London: T. Noble, 1819), 163.

46. J. R. Watson, *The English Hymn: A Critical and Historical Study* (New York: Oxford University Press, 1997), 192.

praise and humility because without God's sustenance his "brittle frame" would surely give way.

> Thy wisdom, pow'r, and goodness, Lord,
>   In all thy works appear:
> And O let man thy praise record;
>   Man, thy distinguish'd care.
>
> From thee the breath of life he drew;
>   That breath thy pow'r maintains;
> Thy tender mercy ever new,
>   His brittle frame sustains.

God's revelation in creation shows that He is not simply the creator of man but also his guardian. Man, witting or unwitting to the perils that loom around him, depends on God for his protection. While it may be easy or tempting for man to neglect the many times he has eluded danger as a result of divine protection, the hymn is a reminder that it is not luck that has preserved him but an omniscient and sovereign God.

> Yet nobler favours claim his praise,
>   Of reason's light possest;
> By revelation's brighter rays
>   Still more divinely blest.
>
> Thy providence, his constant guard
>   When threat'ning woes impend,
> Or will th' impending dangers ward,
>   Or timely succours[47] lend.

Second, God's creation and providence call for the proper response: worship. The final two verses of the hymn offer insightful principles in how to offer God gratitude and praise. The speaker's knowledge of God's goodness compels her to boldly express the gratitude in her heart, for she has a duty to lead others to recognize the same truth. She is to manifest this gratitude in words *and* action to testify to her faith in the goodness of God:

---

47. "Aid, assistance, relief." Johnson, *Dictionary of the English Language*, 181.

On me that providence has shone
  With gentle smiling rays;
O let my lips and life make known
  Thy goodness, and thy praise.

Furthermore, the speaker, as a sinner, will always need the grace of God to help her offer gratitude worthy of being laid down at His altar. Gratitude is not a static entity, a habitual or perfunctory expression performed out of a sense of duty. Gratitude ought to be pure, genuine, and wholehearted. Gratitude ought to continually increase and deepen in the process of maturing in Christ.

Finally, all the things of creation, in all their beauty and splendor, are not merely entities disconnected from the speaker, as if a Creator had fashioned them apart from her, but they are "gifts" created for the speaker to enjoy and look after. Just as God formed them and called them "good," so is the speaker to see creation through His eyes. In the natural world, the speaker is not simply a casual spectator but an intimate participant.

All bounteous Lord, thy grace impart;
  O teach me to improve
Thy gifts with ever grateful heart,
  And crown them with thy love.

Steele explores further many of the themes she alludes to in this hymn in similar hymns, which we will also consider.

Creation as the Revelation of God

Steele's understanding that creation is a revelation of God is expressed powerfully in her hymn "The Voice of the Creatures."[48] Even the title of the hymn depicts the image of creation acting in unison to applaud its Creator. In the first two verses, Steele employs vivid imagery to express how God plainly reveals Himself to the world. First, the presence of God is compared to the brightness of

---

48. Steele, *Poems on Subjects Chiefly Devotional & Miscellaneous Pieces*, Hymn 19, 57–58.

the sun. We can no more fail to witness God's glory than we can see morning's first sign of light. Second, the presence of God is compared to the seemingly infinite coverage of the sun's rays. Steele goes to the extent of personifying the sun—with its bright ray, the sun marks across the sky the signature of the Creator.

> There is a God, all nature speaks,
> Through earth, and air, and seas, and skies:
> See, from the clouds his glory breaks,
> When the first beams of morning rise:
>
> The rising sun, serenely bright,
> O'er the wide world's extended frame,
> Inscribes, in characters of light,
> His mighty Maker's glorious name.

The subsequent four verses implicitly build on the sun metaphor. God, like the sun, grants life to the natural world.

> Diffusing life, his influence spreads,
> And health and plenty smile around,
> And fruitful fields, and verdant meads,
> Are with a thousand blessings crown'd.

The fields and meadows gloriously "shine" because of His goodness and power.

> Almighty goodness, pow'r divine,
> The fields and verdant meads display;
> And bless the hand which made them shine
> With various charms profusely gay.

Man and beast are amply provided for because, like the sun's rays, God is present everywhere, bestowing life to all. Even in the waters below, the sun's effect is seen in its sparkle, depicted in the image of the "crystal flood."

> For man and beast, here daily food
> In wide diffusive plenty grows;
> And there, for drink, the crystal flood
> In streams sweet winding, gently flows.

At the same time, God is more than the sun. He has the power to supply every need of creation. In the verse below, Steele presents a refreshing contrast to the sun: juxtaposed with the nourishing warmth of heated rays is the invigoration of cooling waters.[49]

> By cooling streams, and soft'ning show'rs,
> The vegetable race are fed,
> And trees, and plants, and herbs, and flow'rs,
> Their Maker's bounty smiling spread.

God is therefore plainly revealed in creation through evidence of His provision for it.

The final two verses of the hymn make clear how creation reveals God. Steele points out that no human can attempt to reproduce the beauty that is witnessed in creation. God's beauty is matchless, and any attempt to match it would be in vain. His power and majesty are laid out in creation for all to see, a piercing reality that should inspire "the heart" to acknowledge and surrender to the Creator.

> The flow'ry tribes, all blooming, rise
> Above the faint attempts of art:
> Their bright, inimitable dyes
> Speak sweet conviction to the heart.

Steele openly appeals to every human conscience to recognize this and implores her audience to submit to and worship the Creator. In the previous hymn, the observer, who is intimate with creation, surveys and gazes at it; in the final verse of this hymn, the observer, though curious, merely roams and traces (that is, without direction or meaningful purpose) and has yet to make a committed response. Notice that Steele refrains from using any first-, second-, or third-person pronoun throughout the hymn until the final verse, where she uses the second person to explicitly address the singer/reader.

---

49. Watson highlights the skillful craft of Steele in "finding the correct word or phrase for what she wants to say, and contrasting one element of the hymn with another," as illustrated in this very hymn. Watson, *English Hymn*, 196.

Reaching out to her audience in such a way reveals Steele's clear evangelistic interest.[50] Creation urges every human conscience to come to God, and Steele does not hesitate to do the same.

> Ye curious minds, who roam abroad,
> And trace creation's wonders o'er,
> Confess the footsteps of the God,
> And bow before him, and adore.

Gratitude and Praise as the Proper Response

In Steele's comparatively lengthy hymn titled "A Rural Hymn,"[51] the speaker begins in the first verse by appealing to all creation to render its praise to God, its almighty Creator and Provider. Raise your highest notes of praise, she commands, for He has preserved your being; offer Him your supreme worship, for He is the author of your being. The use of the imperative mood reflects the view that the primary task of earth's creatures is to respond with gratitude and praise.

> To your creator God,
> Your great preserver, raise,
> Ye creatures of his hand,
> Your highest notes of praise:
>   Let ev'ry voice
>   Proclaim his pow'r,
>   His name adore,
>   And loud rejoice.

In the subsequent verse, the praise of creation is distinguished from the praise of man. Man is the crown of creation, so his praise must surpass that of "meaner [lower] ranks." A question that will be

---

50. James notes that while Steele was a Calvinistic Baptist and believed it was divine sovereignty that enabled sinners to respond to the gospel, Steele was not at all diffident in writing about the free offer of the gospel. James, *In Trouble and in Joy*, 154.

51. Steele, *Poems on Subjects Chiefly Devotional & Miscellaneous Pieces*, Hymn 20, 58–63.

considered shortly is why, given that creation is subordinate to man, the natural world is nonetheless implored to be the one to *initiate* praise so that man can follow.

> Let all creation join
> To pay the tribute due;
> Ye meaner ranks begin,
> And man shall learn of you:
> > Let nature raise
> > From ev'ry tongue,
> > A gen'ral song
> > Of grateful praise.

In verses 3 to 14, the imperative mood is maintained as every part of creation is entreated, one after the other, to render its praise to God because of His provision. In succession, each of these verses parallels one another in rhythm and rhyme. By beginning the hymn this way, Steele appears to be painting a portrait of a conductor directing a group of musicians. The conductor passionately seeks to draw out the heart of the song, ensuring that each musician is churning out his best. First the animals are addressed:

> Ye numerous fleecy flocks,
> Far spreading o'er the plain,
> With gentle artless voice
> Assist the humble strain:
> > To give you food,
> > He bids the field
> > Its verdure yield;
> > Extensive good.

> Ye herds of larger size,
> Who feed in meads below,
> Resound your Maker's praise
> In each responsive low:
> > You wait his hand;
> > The herbage grows,
> > The rivulet flows,
> > At his command.

Ye feathered warblers come,
And bring your sweetest lays,
And tune the sprightly song
To your Creator's praise:
 His work you are;
 He tun'd your voice,
 And you rejoice
 Beneath his care.

Then the natural landscape:

Ye trees, which form the shade,
Or bend the loaded bough
With fruits of various kinds,
Your Maker's bounty shew:
 From him you rose;
 Your vernal suits,
 And autumn fruits,
 His hand bestows.

Ye lovely, verdant fields,
In all your green array,
Though silent, speak his praise,
Who makes you bright and gay:
 While we in you,
 With future bread
 Profusely spread,
 His goodness view.

Ye flowers, which blooming shew
A thousand beauteous dyes,
Your sweetest odours breathe,
A fragrant sacrifice,
 To him, whose word
 Gave all your bloom,
 And sweet perfume;
 All-bounteous Lord.

Ye rivers, as you flow,
Convey your Maker's name,
(Where'er you winding rove)
On ev'ry silver stream:
    Your cooling flood,
    His hand ordains
    To bless the plains;
    Great spring of good!

And finally, the forces of nature:

Ye winds, that shake the world
With tempests on your wing,
Or breathe in gentler gales,
To waft the smiling spring;
    Proclaim abroad,
    (As you fulfil
    His sov'reign will)
    The pow'rful God.

Ye clouds, or fraught with show'rs,
Or ting'd with beauteous dyes,
That pour your blessings down,
Or charm our gazing eyes;
    His goodness speak,
    His praise declare,
    As through the air
    You shine or break.

Thou source of light and heat,
Bright sov'reign of the day,
Dispensing blessings round,
With all-diffusive ray;
    From morn to night,
    With ev'ry beam,
    Record his name,
    Who made thee bright.

Fair regent of the night,
With all thy starry train,

> Which rise in shining hosts,
> To gild the azure plain;
>> With countless rays
>> Declare his name,
>> Prolong the theme,
>> Reflect his praise.

The symphony of voices—flock, herd, songbirds, trees, fields, flowers, rivers, winds, clouds, sun, moon—become one in this great hall, the universe.

> Let every creature join
> To celebrate his name,
> And all the various powers
> Assist th' exalted theme.
>> Let nature raise
>> From ev'ry tongue,
>> A gen'ral song
>> Of grateful praise.

Verse 15 signals a dramatic shift in theme: "But oh! from human tongues should nobler praises flow." Recalling Jesus' words in the Sermon on the Mount may perhaps answer the question of why man might learn from the natural world. In Matthew 6, Jesus reminds His disciples of God's knowledge of and care for the natural world. Birds neither sow nor reap, yet God provides for them. Lilies of the field neither toil nor spin, yet God arrays them in glorious beauty. How much more valuable is man? How much more reason should man praise God for His providence? Like the feature soloist in a musical performance, man is therefore directed to rise and give his very best, for all the other players have merely been building up to this anticipated moment:[52]

---

52. The meter applied in this hymn is perceptibly different from Steele's other hymns. Aalders observes that this hymn uses the meter of Psalm 148 in Sternhold and Hopkins's *The Whole Booke of Psalmes* (1562). Aalders, *To Express the Ineffable*, 91. Unlike the "tightly-constructed rhyming couplets," this metre is more free and flexible, beginning with 6.6.6.6., rhyming ABAB, and moving into 4.4.4.4., rhyming CDDC. The purpose of this poetic form is to convey "one long, complicated, joyous, energetic sentence." Watson,

> But oh! from human tongues
> Should nobler praises flow;
> And ev'ry thankful heart,
> With warm devotion glow:
> > Your voices raise,
> > Ye highly blest
> > Above the rest;
> > Declare his praise.

Yet a premium performance cannot be achieved without God's help. The speaker reminds herself that she must rely on God's grace to stir her heart and strengthen her voice. She is confident that upon appealing to God her prayer will be answered. Steele does an exemplary job of tying all the verses together with a single poignant image, which she had been clearly aiming at all along—the image of all creation functioning as a "universal choir." Creation acting together to applaud its Creator is a recurring motif in Steele's hymns that center on the theme of creation.

> Assist me, gracious God,
> My heart, my voice inspire;
> Then shall I grateful join
> The universal choir:
> > Thy grace can raise
> > My heart, my tongue,
> > And tune my song
> > To lively praise.

Gratitude and Praise for All the Contents of Life

Steele's "A Morning Hymn"[53] and "An Evening Hymn"[54] are good gateways into her perspective on the doctrine of providence.

English Hymn, 35. Steele's application of this meter clearly reflects Watson's description of its purpose. For a discussion of meter, see Watson, *English Hymn,* 32–33.

53. Steele, *Poems on Subjects Chiefly Devotional & Miscellaneous Pieces,* Hymn 8, 41–42.

54. Steele, *Poems on Subjects Chiefly Devotional & Miscellaneous Pieces,* Hymn 9, 42–43.

Examined together, the two hymns disclose further insight than each of them alone. Written in the first person, the hymns express Steele's deep personal thoughts on her dependence on God. It is interesting to consider the different ideas that she expresses in each of them and why particular ideas are linked to one hymn and other ideas to the other. After a night of slumber, what should the morning bring? After a day full of activity, what should the evening bring? Have we ever stopped to consider what ought to be the content of our hearts during specific points of the day? Steele offers answers to these questions, illustrated not only in the subject matter of the hymns, but also in their development and structure, attesting to her impressive skill and consciousness as a hymn writer.

The words "morning" and "evening" appearing in the titles of the hymns are not simply a literal or temporal distinction. Figuratively, light conveys states such as hope, renewal, joy, and security, while darkness conveys fear, uncertainty, shame, and sin, all of which are alluded to in these hymns. There is an intentional contrast between how the speakers view and respond to God's provision during the early hours of the morning and in the later hours of the evening.

The emotional and spiritual disposition of the speaker in "A Morning Hymn" is different from that of the speaker in "An Evening Hymn." The speaker in the first verse of "A Morning Hymn" opens with cheerfulness and confidence. Her appeal to God is assured, evident in the use of the superlative; the speaker views God's goodness as unquestionable—both in terms of length of life and content.

> Lord of my life, O may thy praise
> Employ my noblest pow'rs,
> Whose goodness lengthens out my days,
> And fills the circling hours.

In the subsequent verses of the hymn, the speaker's confidence and assurance are maintained. The speaker wakes in the comfort and brightness of her sleeping quarters, and she acknowledges that it is God's provision that has enabled her to do so.

> Perserv'd by thy almighty arm,
>   I pass'd the shades of night,
> Serene, and safe from ev'ry harm,
>   And see returning light.

She does not undermine the value of the simple act of sleep but is instead humbled by it. To be able to sleep without worldly anxieties plaguing the mind is a grace of God, a grace that not all are so fortunate to possess.

> While many spent the night in sighs,
>   And restless pains, and woes;
> In gentle sleep I clos'd my eyes,
>   And undisturb'd repose.

In the fourth verse, sleep is compared to death. In both states of unconsciousness, the body is seen for what it really is—helpless, vulnerable, and fragile.

> When sleep, death's semblance o'er me spread,
>   And I inconscious lay,
> Thy watchful care was round my bed,
>   To guard my feeble clay.

Consequently, the promise that God's provision is present with the speaker, even in her seemingly weakest state, demands her praise.

On the other hand, in the first verse of "An Evening Hymn," the emotional and spiritual disposition of the speaker is much more subdued. Although the speaker still expresses her gratitude, she appeals to God's mercy to guide her in praising God rightfully.

> Great God, to thee my ev'ning song
> With humble gratitude I raise:
> O let thy mercy tune my tongue,
> And fill my heart with lively praise.

Steele's conscious choice of words in the first verses of both hymns moves us to consider the connotations of "gratitude" and "praise." Gratitude refers to a state or feeling, while praise refers to the actual act of worship. We cannot praise God if we are not first grateful. In the first verse of "An Evening Hymn," the speaker is ultimately appealing to God to take her "humble gratitude" and transform it into something more. In the subsequent verses, the speaker willfully calls up reasons that will compel her to praise God more boldly. In verse 2, God is the source of true riches, she among the "craving poor."

> Mercy, that rich unbounded store,
> Does my unnumber'd wants relieve;
> Among thy daily, craving poor,
> On thy all-bounteous hand I live.

In verse 3, God has removed the veil from her eyes, her vision "unclouded" as she beholds His love and power pervading time, every hour a *monument* of grace. The metaphor of the monument reveals the beautiful nature of gratitude: it remembers, it astounds, it endures, it celebrates and honors the one for whom it was built.

> My days unclouded, as they pass,
> And ev'ry gently rolling hour,
> Are monuments of wond'rous grace,
> And witness to thy love and pow'r.

In verse 4, "love and pow'r" is repeated as the speaker strengthens her own assurance in God by considering what she has to fear if God is her protector.

> Thy love and pow'r, (celestial guard)
> Preserve me from surrounding harms:
> Can danger reach me, while the Lord
> Extends his kind protecting arms?

In verse 5, she acknowledges that God knows her wants before she even makes them known to Him.

> My num'rous wants are known to thee,
> Ere my slow wishes can arise;
> Thy goodness measureless and free,
> Is ready still with full supplies.

Using such words as "daily," "days," "gently rolling hour," and "slow wishes" in verses 2 to 5, Steele effectively slows down time, preventing the impulse to move forward too quickly and not look back. It is tempting to reduce our days to a series of routine or inconsequential events, as if God were not directly involved in them. In the above verses, however, Steele reminds us that come evening it is our duty to reflect on the day passed so we can summon up reasons to be thankful for His provision.

The conclusions of both hymns are equally eye-opening. Steele's "A Morning Hymn" ends rather swiftly. While it begins by describing the speaker's thankfulness for God having preserved her in the night and allowing her to be greeted by the morning, it ends with an appeal to God to continue to do so in daylight. Perhaps the image of the speaker in her sleeping (portrayed in the earlier part of this hymn) can be compared to the image of the speaker in her waking (portrayed in the verse below): not only in sleep is the speaker vulnerable to danger, but also in wakefulness. Even when fully conscious, the speaker's perspective is surely limited when compared to the omniscience of God.

> O let the same almighty care
> 　My waking hours attend;
> From ev'ry danger, ev'ry snare,
> 　My heedless steps defend.

The final verse of "A Morning Hymn" reveals the hymn's circular structure. While in the first verse the speaker *looks back* on her days and hours and praises God for His goodness, in the final verse the speaker *looks ahead* and commits her future days to God, even reducing the days to minutes. The first and final verses therefore parallel one another in thought and demonstrate how the speaker depends on the grace of God to sustain her spirit of gratitude and praise as much in the future as in the present.

> Smile on my minutes as they roll,
> 　And guide my future days;
> And let thy goodness fill my soul
> 　With gratitude and praise.

In "An Evening Hymn," as might be expected, the theme is developed more deeply. The speaker, confronting the darkness that evening brings, is likewise confronted with the darkness within her. Having appealed to God's mercy for guidance in offering proper praise, and having consciously recalled the goodness manifested in her life, the speaker then confesses that in her wretchedness she has not always done this. It is important to consider the point that Steele makes here in verse 6: ungratefulness is a sin.[55] While the speaker's faith ought to cause her to give glory to God, her sinfulness causes her to go astray.

> And yet this thoughtless, wretched heart,
> Too oft regardless of thy love,
> Ungrateful, can from thee depart,
> And fond of trifles vainly rove.

It is not until the speaker finds herself in deep reflection (once again, the act of reflection is stressed here) that she sees her own waywardness. In the earlier part of the hymn, the speaker requests God to transform her "humble gratitude" to praise; in the latter part of the hymn, the speaker's request is much more severe—she implores God to bring her to repentance. An ungrateful heart can be restored only by the grace of God.

> When calm reflection finds a place,
> How vile this wretched heart appears!
> O let thy all-subduing grace
> Melt it in penitential tears.

---

55. Consider Steele's poem, "Ingratitude Reproved," in *Poems on Subjects Chiefly Devotional & Miscellaneous Pieces*, 271:

> Your constant task, unweary'd, you pursue,
> Nor deviate from the path your Maker drew.

> My God, shall ev'ry creature join
> In praises to thy glorious name,
> And this ungrateful heart of mine
> Refuse the universal theme?

Expressed in the subsequent verse is the speaker's knowledge that only by the blood of Jesus can restoration take effect. God's highest provision, therefore, is Christ Himself.

> Seal my forgiveness in the blood
> Of Jesus: his dear name alone
> I plead for pardon, gracious God,
> And kind acceptance at thy throne.

It is not merely the divine provision of the basic necessities of life that best meets the human condition, but also the divine provision of redemption through Christ. The speaker is able to fall asleep in peace come evening because she has been delivered from the awful grip of sin.

> Let this blest hope my eyelids close,
> With sleep refresh my feeble frame;
> Safe in thy care may I repose,
> And wake with praises to thy name.

In both hymns, the freedom to sleep in peace is a result beyond the deliverance from external conflict; it is nothing less than a product of being delivered from internal conflict. The weight of sin on our souls has far more destructive consequences. In this final verse of "An Evening Hymn," the disposition of the speaker, upon the realization of what Christ has done for her, remarkably resembles the speaker in "A Morning Hymn," who wakes up full of hope and anticipation.

Jesus Christ—God's Highest Provision

Christ as God's highest provision is a prominent theme in Steele's hymns. In "Praise to God for the Blessings of Providence and Grace,"[56] this truth becomes central as the speaker contemplates the providence of God. The first seven verses record the speaker's consideration of how God has preserved her. They depict the journey

---

56. Steele, *Poems on Subjects Chiefly Devotional & Miscellaneous Pieces*, Hymn 22, 65–67.

of life—from birth until death—every "rolling year" testifying to untold blessings.

> Almighty Father, gracious Lord,
>   Kind guardian of my days,
> Thy mercies let my heart record
>   In songs of grateful praise.
>
> In life's first dawn, my tender frame
>   Was thy indulgent care,
> Long ere I could pronounce thy name
>   Or breathe the infant prayer.
>
> When reason with my stature grew,
>   How weak her brightest ray!
> How little of my God I knew!
>   How apt from thee to stray!
>
> Around my path what dangers rose!
>   What snares spread all the road!
> No power could guard me from my foes,
>   But my preserver, God.
>
> When life hung trembling on a breath,
>   'Twas thy almighty love
> That sav'd me from impending death,
>   And bade my fears remove.
>
> How many blessings round me shone
>   Where'er I turn'd my eye!
> How many pass'd almost unknown,
>   Or unregarded, by.
>
> Each rolling year new favours brought
>   From thy exhaustless store:
> But ah! in vain my labouring thought
>   Would count thy mercies o'er.

The eighth verse (which is also, interestingly enough, precisely the midpoint of the hymn) alludes to the greatest blessing of them all—the grace offered through the sacrifice of God's Son.[57]

> While sweet reflection, through my days
> 　Thy bounteous hand would trace;
> Still dearer blessings claim my praise,
> 　The blessings of thy grace.

Prior to identifying Jesus, however, Steele first points to Scripture as the source that makes this truth known. Knowledge of all that God provides is not hidden, for God has revealed this in His Word.

> Yes, I adore thee, gracious Lord,
> 　For favours more divine;
> That I have known thy sacred word,
> 　Where all thy glories shine.

As the speaker contemplates the blessing of Jesus, she is profoundly humbled by His death and sacrifice. In verse 10 below, the parenthetical exclamation reinforces the speaker's emotional state. Jesus' death is no doubt an act of "almighty love," but for humankind such sacrificial love is nonetheless shocking given that His death was for the salvation of sinners, hence the speaker's response, "surprizing scene!" The shock value is reinforced by emphatic repetition, "for man, lost man, to die."[58] According to Watson, the

---

57. A hymn that expresses the same theme is "The Goodness of God," in Steele, *Poems on Subjects Chiefly Devotional & Miscellaneous Pieces*, Hymn 46, 98. Both these hymns teach that worship of God must always be Christ-centered, for the greatest reason to praise God is Christ Himself. In "The Goodness of God," the third verse expresses a similar idea:

> He gave his son, his only son,
> 　To ransom rebel worms;
> 'Tis here he makes his goodness known
> 　In its divinest forms.

58. Aalders notes that the repetition here "causes the singer to linger over the cause of Christ's death, acknowledging her own role in requiring this sacrifice." Aalders, *To Express the Ineffable*, 164.

seemingly contrary ideas in the form of parenthetical exclamation—
"(Almighty love!" and "surprizing scene!)"—are devices that Steele
typically uses to present a single event observed from two different
perspectives.[59]

> 'Tis here, I view with pleasing pain,
>   How Jesus left the sky,
> (Almighty love! surprizing scene!)
>   For man, lost man, to die.

In humility, the speaker is compelled to praise God for this
blessing. The speaker's conjured image of Christ transports her to
a higher state.

> When blest with that transporting view,
>   That Jesus died for me,
> For this sweet hope what praise is due,
>   O God of grace, to thee!
>
> And may I hope that Christ is mine?
>   That source of ev'ry bliss,
> That noblest gift of love divine—
>   What wond'rous grace is this!

Yet with this image in mind, human praise sinks to a lower plane,
since even the most passionate human praise cannot match this act
of divine love. Such praise is only possible in the heavenly realm.

> My highest praise, alas, how poor!
>   How cold my warmest love!
> Dear Saviour, teach me to adore
>   As angels do above.
>
> But frail mortality in vain
>   Attempts the blissful song;
> The high, the vast, the boundless strain,
>   Claims an immortal tongue.

---

59. Watson, *English Hymn,* 193.

The final verses of the hymn express the speaker's longing for the moment when she, at last, is able to praise God in the way she was created. Beyond the universal choir of the earth, praise for the blessings of God's providence and grace will come to those who will one day stand in His glory.

> Lord, when this mortal frame decays,
>   And ev'ry weakness dies,
> Complete the wonders of thy grace,
>   And raise me to the skies.
>
> Then shall my joyful pow'rs unite,
>   In more exalted lays,
> And join the happy sons of light,
>   In everlasting praise.

Gratitude and Praise for the Unknown

In Steele's hymn "The Mysteries of Providence,"[60] another important insight emerges. Beholding the beauty of God's creation and receiving the blessings of God's providence should elicit trust in Him even amid the unknown. There remains great mystery as to *how* God operates among us, yet we know that He upholds and protects the universe, sustains it by natural laws, works together with secondary powers to cause things to happen as they ought, and sovereignly rules it. Our limited perspective of His ways is a result of our finitude, being human and sinful.

> Lord, how mysterious are thy ways!
> How blind are we! how mean our praise!
> Thy steps can mortal eyes explore?
> 'Tis ours, to wonder and adore.
>
> Thy deep decrees from creature sight
> Are hid in shades of awful night;
> Amid the lines, with curious eye,
> Not angel minds presume to pry.

---

60. Steele, *Poems on Subjects Chiefly Devotional & Miscellaneous Pieces*, Hymn 72, 131–32.

While it may be natural to wonder at certain points of our lives about our future, the speaker in this hymn is not restless to find out: she has come to entrust her years ahead into God's hands, whether that future be blissful or painful. The speaker is able to do so because she knows that her God is a God of love—should suffering ensue, in due time the ways of her Creator will be made known.

> Great God, I would not ask to see
> What in futurity shall be;
> If light and bliss attend my days,
> Then let my future hours be praise.
>
> Is darkness and distress my share?
> Then let me trust thy guardian care;
> Enough for me, if love divine,
> At length through ev'ry cloud shall shine.

More than the desire to know the future, then, is the speaker's desire to know that she belongs to Christ. While the circumstances of life may remain mysterious, the promise of Christ to those who commit their lives to Him is not.

> Yet this my soul desires to know,
> Be this my only wish below,
> "That Christ is mine!"—this great request
> Grant, bounteous God,—and I am blest.[61]

Conclusion

The hymns examined in this chapter illustrate how Steele saw the glory of God in creation, in the everyday, amid life's seeming ordinariness. Steele was able to do so because she understood the value of solitude, meditation, and prayer. She actively sought God, not just

---

61. Aalders calls attention to Steele's familiar practice of questioning in her hymns. Steele's use of questions to search for meaning expresses a "plaintive and personal" tone. At the same time, the final verse of this hymn expresses assurance: "Steele affirms that she will be content to live in 'darkness and distress' if she could be assured of Christ's love." Aalders, *To Express the Ineffable*, 130–31.

in the immediate visible aspects of life, but also in the aspects of life that often go unnoticed. The insights drawn from her hymns testify to the fruit of honest, heartfelt, spiritual reflection. In seeking to see God in all of life, Steele above all saw Christ. God's provision of a Savior was the reason for her contentment, hope, joy, and peace and the reason she did not fear the future, as uncertain as it may have been. This was certainly a reality for Steele during her time of trial and suffering, as we shall see in the following chapter.

Let time and circumstance, O gracious God,
be resigned to thy sovereign disposal…
Say to my soul,
'My grace is sufficient for thee,'
and I shall be safe.

CHAPTER THREE

Faith in the Face of Suffering

When it comes to the subject of suffering, one of the most important biblical doctrines to understand is the sovereignty of God—that is, that God has the complete power to exercise His will over creation. Trust in a sovereign God requires a resignation to His will, or, in the words of John Gill, "an entire acquiescence in the will of God in all things, and especially in adverse dispensations of providence, which is a trial of it."[1] While being able to fully resign to the will of God in times of trial can often be challenging, willing what He wills and is pleasing to Him can be seen in the consummate example of Jesus Christ in His suffering, particularly when He had to face what was to transpire on the cross. Even upon knowing that He would have to endure being forsaken by His Father and subjected to His divine wrath on sin, Jesus nonetheless resigned His will to His Father's, praying on the Mount of Olives, "Not my will, but yours, be done."[2]

The process of resigning to the will of God is by the power of divine grace, for it is sin that hardens the heart, making the individual "have no will nor desire to understand what is good, and still less to practice it."[3] By our own human efforts we cannot will or become submissive to the will of God; we must depend on the Spirit of God and the power of His efficacious grace.[4]

---

1. Gill, *Body of Practical Divinity*, 810.
2. Gill, *Body of Practical Divinity*, 810.
3. Gill, *Body of Practical Divinity*, 811.
4. Gill, *Body of Practical Divinity*, 812.

In the face of suffering, Gill reminds us that "every follower of Christ has a cross, his own peculiar cross; which he is to take up willingly and bear cheerfully" (Rom. 12:12).[5] Our willingness to take up the cross, along with all the hardship it entails, is rooted in knowing the sovereign God to whom we answer and His ways. He is a God of love, the source of goodness, the one who leads us onto paths of righteousness:

> Afflictions lie in the way to the heavenly glory, which is a *narrow way*, an afflicted way, strewed with afflictions; and through this rough way all Christian pilgrims and travellers pass, and enter the kingdom; so did Christ himself; and ere long they will come to the end of it, and out of great tribulations, and therefore should patiently endure them. They are no other than fatherly chastisements, given in love, and for good; and sooner or later apparently issue in good, either here or hereafter, and therefore to be yielded to with filial reverence and subjection; and though in themselves not joyous, but grievous; yet since peaceable fruits of righteousness follow them, those who are exercised with them, should be content to bear them.[6]

Like the lament of the psalmist when confronting the seeming absence of God, "Why, O Lord, do you stand far away? Why do you hide yourself in times of trouble?" (Ps. 10:1), these truths become our hope, our lifeline. In such moments our patience is surely exercised, but our faith enables us to quietly wait for God to reveal Himself to us again. At times we may find ourselves impatient, desperate to find a reason behind the suffering, or we may complain about the duration of the suffering, or we may even fall into unbelief, thinking that God has forsaken us. Other times, by God's grace, we find ourselves more patient, more willing to quietly wait on Him (Isa. 8:17; Mic. 7:7–10).[7]

The hymns examined in this chapter will demonstrate how Steele's experiences reflect those Gill described. Steele knew she

---

5. Gill, *Body of Practical Divinity*, 816.
6. Gill, *Body of Practical Divinity*, 816.
7. Gill, *Body of Practical Divinity*, 817.

answered to a sovereign God and recognized that it was her sin that prevented her from fully worshiping Him. Her hymns express the two sides of the journey—one that exposed her doubts, and the other, her faith.

Trials in the Life of Anne Steele

During the latter part of the seventeenth century, the Church of England took control of religious life in Britain. Those who remained part of the English church were to conform to its doctrines and practices; those failing to were ultimately driven out. These were the Nonconformists (or Dissenters), who, as a matter of conscience, chose to worship outside the state church:

> In the very act of Dissenting, these Christians made a statement about an established church which they considered too implicated in an 'uncritiqued' world, a state church enmeshed with monarch and Parliament, which tried to dictate how all Christians in Britain should worship and structure their churches. Thus, the Nonconformists both rejected the established church and were themselves rejected by it.[8]

As a result, the Dissenters were subject to ruthless persecution as Parliament passed a series of penal laws intended to subvert their power.[9] As Baptists, many of Steele's ancestors were among those

---

8. Jane Shaw, "Introduction: Why 'Culture and the Nonconformist Tradition'?," in *Culture and the Nonconformist Tradition*, ed. Jane Shaw and Alan Kreider (Cardiff: University of Wales Press, 1999), 2.

9. The 1661 Corporation Act required all municipal officials to take Communion according to the rites of the Church of England. The 1662 Act of Uniformity forced all ministers to accede to the Book of Common Prayer and use it in their religious services; approximately two thousand clergymen refusing to comply (opposing its "unreformed and superstitious elements") were ejected from the Church of England. The 1664 Conventicle Act forbade any meeting for worship comprising more than four people (excluding those in the household). The 1665 Five Mile Act prohibited any minister from approaching five miles of a town where he had formerly ministered, thereby preventing him from coming in contact with his former congregation. Dewey D. Wallace, "English Calvinism in a New Era," in *Shapers of English Calvinism, 1660–1714:*

persecuted. Dissenters had to hold meetings in secret; informers were rampant; guards were put on watch to alert others of danger; ministers caught preaching faced heavy fines and even imprisonment.

In 1751 John Gill wrote *The Dissenters' Reasons for Separating from the Church of England* to address the Anglicans' charge against the Dissenters for stirring up strife between them. Gill responded by declaring that the Church of England was not a model of the true church because it did not align its doctrines and practices with Scripture. The Dissenters chose to be independent of the state church because they desired a church that was founded on the laws of God and not of man. They upheld Reformed principles and Calvinistic doctrine[10] and denounced the preaching of mere morality and salvation achieved by personal merit. They believed in proper administration of baptism and the Lord's Supper. Baptism was to be performed by immersion and for professed believers only (contrary to infants baptized by sprinkling),[11] and the Lord's Supper was

---

Variety, Persistence, and Transformation (New York: Oxford University Press, 2011), 21–22. See "An Age of Intolerance (1645–1688)" in Broome's *Bruised Reed*, 13–40, for a detailed background on how these circumstances affected Steele's ancestors.

10. Associated with the French Reformer John Calvin (1509–1564), Calvinistic doctrine was based on the ideas emerging from the early Reformation. Among its doctrinal beliefs was what came known to be the five points of Calvinism: total depravity, unconditional election (predestination), limited atonement, irresistible grace, and perseverance of the saints. "These points were a kind of carapace surrounding and protecting the softer body of Reformed religiosity and teaching, which consisted of an overwhelming sense of divine sovereignty and of the pure gratuitousness of the saving grace of God, both of which were soteriological in focus." In the latter half of the seventeenth century, Calvinism was linked particularly to the Dissenters. Wallace, "English Calvinism in a New Era," 13, 19.

11. While Baptists acknowledged "their belief that only adult believers who gave evidence of an experiential faith are proper candidates for baptism, Calvinistic Baptists also maintained that baptism was linked to the experience of regeneration. However, what they always vigorously affirmed was that the waters of baptism were not in themselves efficacious for salvation, but rather *signified* that the person had already been regenerated. Moreover, while they emphasized that baptism was never to be seen as merely a rite of initiation or

reserved for members or associated members. They believed in exercising discipline in the church so that only the regenerate were part of it. The life testimony of its members was to be a genuine reflection of the teachings of Christ.[12]

While much suffering ensued as a result of their separation, in other ways the life of the Dissenters thrived. For one, the response of the Dissenters to the ongoing persecution showed how firm they were in holding fast to their convictions. Knowing that there were informers among them who would report their activities to authorities, the Porton/Broughton Church[13] (the church of Steele's ancestors) responded to the persecution by increasing church discipline. They were "very conscious that, while it was being constantly watched and persecuted, informers would glory in demonstrating that it was harbouring worldly and licentious people. So for the cohesion and strength of the persecuted body, strong discipline was maintained. It was in fact a spiritual strength for the church."[14]

---

a means of entry into membership of the church, it was accepted nevertheless as a real sign of fellowship with Christ and with his body, the Church." Karen Smith, "The Covenant Life of Some Eighteenth-Century Calvinistic Baptists in Hampshire and Wiltshire," in *Pilgrim Pathways: Essays in Baptist History in Honour of B. R. White*, ed. William H. Brackney, Paul S. Fiddes, and John H. Y. Briggs (Macon, Ga.: Mercer University Press, 1999), 175.

12. John Gill, *The Dissenters' Reasons for Separating from the Church of England*, 4th ed. (London, 1760). Wallace highlights the spiritual intimacy that existed in the dissenting community: "The dissenting religious community, especially the more orthodox and Calvinist part of it…developed a fairly homogenized culture of the conventicle or gathered community that was centered on warm and edifying fellowship within their congregations, 'walking together' in the ways of the Lord and eschewing worldliness. They could enforce within the confines of these congregations a degree of voluntary discipline unworkable in a parish system and enjoy the long sermons of 'affectionate' pastors who supplemented their sermons with a steady diet of spiritual discourse and exhortation in more personal settings." Wallace, "English Calvinism in a New Era," 26–27.

13. The Baptist church resided in Porton and later settled in Broughton.

14. Broome, *Bruised Reed*, 35–36. The Dissenters were committed to the primary role of Scripture and the "transformative role of doctrine in the Christian's life." Aalders, *To Express the Ineffable*, 41.

Although the Glorious Revolution of 1688 and the Toleration Act of 1689 eventually allowed Dissenters to worship freely, they still faced some restrictions until the nineteenth century. By law they were excluded from involvement in England's civil and political life, attending universities, and entering specific professions. These restrictions led to the establishment of dissenting academies, and Dissenters such as Steele's father and brother went into business and trade and did so profitably. So in spite of the barriers they faced, the Steele family and others were nonetheless able to "direct their energies toward self-education and business and were quite as rich and cultured as many of their aristocratic contemporaries."[15]

Nonconformist life also influenced the literary sphere where Steele came into prominence. Being part of a persecuted group of Christians contributed to shaping her: "Steele's efforts as a writer likely were bolstered by a more fundamental identification with the Dissenting church, which was characterized by a common sense of oppression."[16] Such a context lent a distinctive tone to her writing, one marked by spiritual passion, prudence, and probing. The life of nonconformity brought forth a "stimulus to the pen and [an] instinct to preserve its own identity through its history. The culture of dissenting groups does, indeed, seem to have made them (for members of their social class) unusually articulate, theologically aware and ready with their pens."[17]

---

15. Broome, *Bruised Reed*, 126. Describing the educational context, Wallace writes, "Some of the best scholarship and theological inquiry of the time flowed from dissenting pens. The dissenting academies which provided education for those to whom the universities were closed became centers of a more innovative and modern education than was often to be found in the older academic institutions." Wallace, "English Calvinism in a New Era," 27.

16. Aalders, *To Express the Ineffable*, 23.

17. Reeves, *Pursuing the Muses: Female Education and Nonconformist Culture*, 5. Interesting to note is how Steele's being part of the dissenting group opened up opportunities for her as a female hymn writer: "Whereas long-established social and theological scruples obstructed women's access to public discourses, during the eighteenth century poetry and hymnody became increasingly seen as acceptable modes of public expression for women." This

Steele was brought up in a family of Dissenters. Her father was a Particular Baptist minister and her mother, Anne (née Froude), was the daughter of a Particular Baptist minister. Sadly, in 1720, at the age of thirty-six, Steele's mother died after giving birth to her third child, Thomas, who died a month later. When their mother died, Steele's older brother, William, and she were five and three years old. In 1723, Steele's father remarried to a woman named Anne (née Cator) whose family were also Particular Baptists. In 1724, another baby girl, Mary, arrived in the family.

Much of the information about the Steele household comes from the diary of Steele's stepmother, in which she wrote on a daily basis from the time of her marriage to William until her death in 1760. Concerning its breadth and quality Broome writes, "There can be few eighteenth-century diaries to equal them in content, duration and spirituality."[18] These entries offer a more personal look at Steele's life, especially the ill health she had to endure for much of it.

Steele became a victim of malaria at a young age. It was a common disease that frequently affected those living in marshy environments, such as where Steele resided by the River Wallop in the south of England. In 1731 when Steele was fourteen, during a time when she was feeling especially weak, Mrs. Steele revealed her thoughts and feelings concerning the physical and spiritual state of her stepdaughter: "[I] cry earnestly on Anne's account that as God has been pleased to make her sensible of the want and worth of a Saviour, so he would also give her a well-grounded hope that she have an interest in that Saviour that so she might be happy here

---

was especially true for Dissenters: "Women were already operating beyond the bounds of propriety; that is, in accepting the Dissenting cause, they had already questioned established assumptions about what was correct moral and spiritual behavior. It was in this context that Anne Steele composed and published her hymns." Aalders, *To Express the Ineffable*, 51–52. Other female hymn writers whom Aalders describes here are Elizabeth Singer Rowe (1674–1737) and Anne Dutton (1692–1765). See Aalders, *To Express the Ineffable*, 52–57.

18. Broome, *Bruised Reed*, 177.

and forever."[19] Sometime later, when Steele's condition still did not improve, Mrs. Steele expressed her apprehension: "I beg the affliction may be sanctified to her and that her life may be spared."[20] Months following the initial occurrence of Steele's illness, Mrs. Steele noted a development in the circumstances: "I have great hope that God have indeed begun to work upon the souls of our children."[21]

It is clear that Mrs. Steele possessed a strong Christian spirit and that she hungered and watched carefully for her children's profession of faith in Christ. Her prayers were soon answered. The illness that her stepdaughter had suffered the preceding year moved her to reflect on life's weightier matters: "Anne's long illness in the previous autumn had been used for her soul's good and that the great issues of eternity had weighed in her soul as her strength appeared to be ebbing away."[22] At the age of fifteen, Steele made the decision to be baptized.[23]

---

19. Broome, *Bruised Reed*, 79.

20. Broome, *Bruised Reed*, 79.

21. Broome, *Bruised Reed*, 79–80. It is interesting to note how Mrs. Steele saw the whole process of an individual's coming to faith and desiring church membership. Smith writes, "Since acceptance into a congregation was dependent on the individual's ability to give a sure testimony, efforts were made to ensure that the testimony of those received was real and genuine, and that the person was of sound character. After the testimony was 'given in' to the congregation, neighbors and relatives gave statements regarding the character of the individual. Then following discussion, a vote was taken by church members to decide whether the person should be accepted. Those speaking on behalf of a person seeking membership took their responsibility seriously." In 1755, for example, Mrs. Steele shared in her diary that she had given advice to a woman who was seeking to be baptized and had told her that, though she hoped God had "been at work upon her soul," to "wait a little longer and be constant in prayer for more knowledge and faith and also to count the cost of a profession of religion then if it appears to be a work of grace upon her heart it will be no grief of mind to her to wait God's time." *Diaries of Anne [Cator] Steele*, vol. 5 (January 4, 1755), Angus Library, Regent's Park College, Oxford; quoted in Smith, "The Covenant Life of Some Eighteenth-Century Calvinistic Baptists," 172–73.

22. Broome, *Bruised Reed*, 81.

23. Many years later, upon the end of her life, Mrs. Steele could thankfully declare: "I have no greater joy than to know that my children walk in the

Steele's ill health is often the focus of biographical sketches of her. Her biographers' consensus that she was not shaken by her ongoing suffering and remained devoted to God speaks volumes about her faith. In the preface of the 1780 posthumous publication of Steele's *Miscellaneous Pieces in Verse and Prose*, Caleb Evans praised Steele for her capacity to exude joy even in the midst of affliction: "She possessed a native cheerfulness of disposition, which not even the uncommon and agonizing pains she endured in the latter part of her life could deprive her of. In every short interval of abated suffering, she would in a variety of ways, as well as by her enlivening conversation, give pleasure to all around her."

Steele's physical pain would have been interminable and excruciating given the time she lived in: "Before the Victorian era, medicine had but paltry power to cure disease and save the sick, and few entertained great expectations of it."[24] Remedies for infectious diseases and alleviation of pain were virtually nonexistent. Malaria was a debilitating disease:

---

truth." *Diaries of Anne [Cator] Steele*, vol. 5 (June 26, 1758), Angus Library, Regent's Park College, Oxford; quoted in Broome, *Bruised Reed*, 146.

See Broome, *Bruised Reed*, 79–82 for a description of Steele's baptismal experience. Here Broome notes that sadly there is no record of Steele's testimony, yet he writes, "But when we come to examine the hymns that Anne later wrote, we shall see that much of her spiritual experience lies embedded in them."

Smith's essay, which focuses on Steele's church, demonstrates how an individual's faith is cultivated and shared in the context of the church. Steele's decision to be baptized demonstrated her firm commitment to the faith. Smith writes, "Membership in a particular 'gathered community' of believers was not a matter of merely giving verbal assent to a covenant agreement, but rather was dependent upon the individual's ability to demonstrate a sincere commitment to the Lord Jesus based on his or her knowledge and experience of Christ in Scripture." Upon being baptized, members were to give a testimony of their "experience" to members of the congregation: "No one was to be baptized and received into church membership without having first made public profession of an 'experience of grace,' or without showing clear signs of living in obedience to the commands set forth in Scripture and exemplified in the life of Christ." Smith, "The Covenant Life of Some Eighteenth-Century Calvinistic Baptists," 170.

24. Roy Porter, "What Is Disease?" in *The Cambridge History of Medicine*, ed. Roy Porter (New York: Cambridge University Press, 2006), 95.

[Malaria] was a disease which the people of the marshes permanently had to live with until they succumbed to its frequent attacks or died of secondary causes. Its course was complicated by its interaction with many other prevailing infections of the time.... It was a disease which also appears to have set up a sequence of consequences and circumstances which fed deeper into the spiral of sickness and death.[25]

The onset of other infections escalated the condition of a victim suffering from malaria, to the point that "its long continuance [was] apt to impair their constitutions, and to produce obstinate chronicle distempers."[26] Moreover, the victim would undoubtedly suffer from a lack of physical energy as a result of its associated anemia and poor diet.[27]

Steele's prose articulates her perspective on suffering. As her observers have noted, one aspect of Steele's writing that elicits such emotion is her honesty. Being able to read a personal account of her suffering enables us to not only sympathize with her, but also to

---

25. Mary J. Dobson, *Contours of Death and Disease in Early Modern England*, Cambridge Studies in Population, Economy and Society in Past Time (Cambridge: Cambridge University Press, 1997), 342. The possibility of contracting other infections was a real threat for Steele. Broome notes a smallpox outbreak in Broughton in the summer of 1759: "Many died from it and on 20th July the church had a special prayer meeting on account of it. Anne was ill at the time and greatly feared catching it in her weak condition." Broome, *Bruised Reed*, 144.

26. James Lind, "An Essay on Diseases Incidental to Europeans in Hot Climates. With the Method of Preventing Their Fatal Consequences" (London: T. Becket, 1777), 303, quoted in Dobson, *Contours of Death and Disease*, 330. Later in life, Steele experienced stomach troubles (as a result of either peptic ulceration or irritable bowel syndrome), shortness of breath (as a result of coronary insufficiency or repeated tract infections, chronic bronchitis, or recurrent attacks of pleurisy), and severe toothaches. Broome recaps the diagnosis of a consultant pathologist who examines Steele's symptoms. Broome, *Bruised Reed*, 79. For this pathologist's description of Steele's condition, see Michael F. Dixon and Hugh F. Steele-Smith, "Anne Steele's Health: A Modern Diagnosis," *Baptist Quarterly* 32 (July 1988): 351–56.

27. Dobson, *Contours of Death and Disease*, 338.

better appreciate how she develops a perception of it. For instance, her prose work "Thoughts in Sickness, and on Recovery" shows how her physical condition disrupted her everyday life:

> The first attacks of a fever have so weakened my nerves and spirits, that every sprightly faculty and almost every cheerful thought is sunk in a stupid languor; a listless inattention even to common things overspreads me, conversation is tasteless, and reading and thinking almost impracticable. But alas, this is not the worst! The bounties of providence and the blessings of grace hardly excite a grateful thought, or quicken a warm desire—wretched state![28]

Steele reveals the causes of her distress. Not only did her illness affect her physically but also emotionally, psychologically, and spiritually. She found it challenging to have energy or enthusiasm to engage in even the most mundane activity, much less the activities she most enjoyed. Her greatest concern, however, was that fatigue and weariness robbed her of her ability to easily recall the divine goodness, the abundant gifts and grace of God. Yet Steele did not use her suffering as an excuse to neglect God. She attributed her lethargic state to her mortal body, which, "frail and disordered," was vulnerable to the trials of life: "Of what a feeble texture is this mortal tabernacle! and how much is the tenant mind (though of an immortal nature) pained and depressed by its weakness, and hurt by the storms which shake the tottering frame!"[29] Because Steele was highly conscious of this weakness and its effects on her, she knew it was her duty to summon up the things of God:

> Am I enough awake to feel my chains, and yet not wish for liberty? Let me try to rouse myself from this lethargy of the mind, and if I cannot look forward through the gloom which hangs so heavy on my intellectual sight, let me look back and try to recover some little remembrance of past scenes. Shall

---

28. Steele, *Miscellaneous Pieces in Verse and Prose by Theodosia*, included in Broome, *Bruised Reed*, 342.

29. Broome, *Bruised Reed*, 342.

the immortal spirit united to this frail disordered body be so much influenced by its weakness, as if it were to sink with it into the common earth? Think, O my soul, hadst thou not once nobler views and brighter hopes?[30]

Steele knew to remember her former days in which God had providentially delivered her from suffering.[31] Her endeavors to ponder the things of God, even in her ailing and anguished state, are apparent in her hymns. As the subsequent section will demonstrate, much can be learned from the way Steele sought to rise above her difficult circumstances.

---

30. Broome, *Bruised Reed*, 342.

31. Consider the following excerpt from one of Steele's poems, "Wrote in an Ill State of Health in the Spring," in *Poems on Subjects Chiefly Devotional & Miscellaneous Pieces*, 278–80, where she describes her despondent state:

> To me 'tis all a blank! untouch'd my soul
> With nature's harmony! my eyes, uncharm'd
> With all her beauties, cannot find a joy
> In the once lovely, once delightful scene!
> A gloom of sadness hangs upon my spirits,
> And prompts the frequent sigh and silent tear.
> Depress'd by pain and sickness, all my powers
> Are dull and languid, every joy is tasteless;
> All nature fades, and pleasure is no more!
>
> Ah! what is life, so lov'd, so dearly priz'd,
> If health be absent? 'tis a ling'ring night
> Of tedious expectation, spent in sighs,
> And restless wishes for the cheerful dawn.

Steele concludes the poem by reminding herself that gratitude ought not to be limited by her condition ("Nor let the grateful rapture be confin'd"):

> To that almighty goodness, which bestows
> Its gifts unmeasur'd, undeserv'd, on me.
> Nor let the grateful rapture be confin'd;
> Since o'er the whole creation wide diffus'd,
> Divine beneficence unbounded smiles,
> And claims the tribute of unbounded praise.

Suffering and the Sovereignty of God in Anne Steele's Hymns

Reliance on the Grace of God to Inspire True Worship

In the hymn "Imploring Divine Influences,"[32] Steele points out the futility in attempting to worship God by human effort. Only by turning to God could she break from the pull of human influence—of pride, indolence, and inconstancy—to move to the divine. In verses 1 and 2 of the hymn, even the loftiest of human efforts cause the speaker to plunge further into insipidness. The depths are certainly low, for the speaker sinks to "earth" and is "low in dust." The verb "sink" in verse 2 portrays the powerlessness of the speaker to rise from where she is. And yet the sinking is necessary: only in this state can the speaker be lifted up—by the grace of God. The resulting image in verse 3 is a convicting one: "The sinner prostrate at thy feet."

> My God, whene'er my longing heart
> Thy praiseful tribute would impart,
> In vain my tongue with feeble aim,
> Attempts the glories of thy name.
>
> In vain my boldest thoughts arise,
> I sink to earth and lose the skies;
> Yet I may still thy grace implore,
> And low in dust thy name adore.
>
> O let thy grace my heart inspire
> And raise each languid, weak desire;
> Thy grace, which condescends to meet
> The sinner prostrate at thy feet.

Only in this condition is the speaker aware of her own insufficiency. She must fall on her knees in humility and submission in order to be in a place where she can love, adore, and enjoy her God.

> With humble fear let love unite,
> And mix devotion with delight;

---

32. Steele, *Poems on Subjects Chiefly Devotional & Miscellaneous Pieces*, Hymn 2, 26–27.

> Then shall thy name be all my joy,
> Thy praise, my constant blest employ.

In the subsequent verse, the God who at first seemed to occupy the lofty skies has become the one who "looks kindly" on her condition. The speaker imagines the glorious worship that takes place in the skies and trusts in God's power to also guide her toward such divine worship.[33]

> Thy name inspires the harps above
> With harmony, and praise, and love;
> That grace, which tunes th' immortal strings,
> Looks kindly down on mortal things.

In the final verse, God reveals Himself to her, and fruit is evident in her worship. By relying on the grace of God, the speaker's worship has become sincere, pleasing, and above all properly centered:

> O let thy grace guide ev'ry song,
> And fill my heart and tune my tongue;
> Then shall the strain harmonious flow,
> And heav'n's sweet work begin below.

Faith…in the Midst of God's Silence

The silence of God in times of suffering can lead to despair, and Steele's experience was not the exception. Aalders observes that Steele's writing shows her awareness of God's response to her experience of suffering, and this response was one of "absence and silence, negations that would complicate her attempts to make affirmations about God and the spiritual life."[34] Aalders believes that the crucial question emerging from Steele's writing is, "If God is a loving God, as she faithfully affirms that he is, why does she experience this physical and emotional anguish? And why, she asks, as so many have asked,

---

33. Aalders observes that this verse shows a contrast between "flawed mortal praise" and the "immortal praise which is so much closer to the source of its inspiration." Aalders, *To Express the Ineffable*, 95.

34. Aalders, *To Express the Ineffable*, 112.

is God silent in the face of that suffering?"[35] A close look at two of Steele's hymns will shed light on how she probes the answer to this question and uncovers the proper response.

In Steele's hymn "Absence from God,"[36] the speaker begins by describing her knowledge of God's mercy and grace. The choice of words in verse 1 evokes an intimate image of God. God's mercy is "tender," His comfort "indulgent." The anthropomorphic references reinforce this. The image portrayed in the first verse is very much like that of a father caring for his child: God is so close that He can *hear* the sigh of His child, so close that He can *wipe* the tears from His child's eyes.

> O thou, whose tender mercy hears
>   Contrition's humble sigh;
> Whose hand, indulgent, wipes the tears
>   From sorrow's weeping eye:

Yet, at the moment, the speaker feels distant from God. The contrast between verse 1 and the rest of the hymn is stark—the former depicting a warm image of God, the latter a cold one. In fact, the final line of verse 1 is punctuated with a colon, signaling that the thought is incomplete.

A sudden interruption in verse 2 ("See!") reflects the fretful state of the speaker and her yearning to seize God's attention. The image is a poignant one: the speaker is hanging low before God's throne; she is lost and desperate to hear the voice of her Father.

> See! Low before thy throne of grace,
>   A wretched wand'rer mourn;
> Hast thou not bid me seek thy face?
>   Has thou not said, Return?

Having once basked in her Father's protection, the speaker describes how terrified she is of being cast away. Interestingly enough the

---

35. Aalders, *To Express the Ineffable*, 113.

36. Steele, *Poems on Subjects Chiefly Devotional & Miscellaneous Pieces*, Hymn 60, 115–16.

speaker sees herself as the root of the problem. If she is driven away from God's throne of grace, it is a result of her not trusting in His grace enough.

> And shall my guilty fears prevail
>   To drive me from thy feet?
> O let not this dear refuge fail,
>   This only safe retreat.

The seeming absence of God is depicted by the imagery of absolute darkness. The speaker's lonely world is so dark that not even a single ray of light exists.

> Absent from thee, my guide, my light,
>   Without one cheering ray,
> Through dangers, fears, and gloomy night,
>   How desolate my way!

At the same time, the speaker does not lose faith in God. She appeals to God to shine His light once again in her life. The speaker has endured great suffering, yet even in the face of God's silence, she nonetheless believes in His power to return to her and restore her condition. Her appeal earns our sympathy, for her request is a humble one—she simply wants a "taste" of the joy that only her God is able to supply her.

> O shine on this benighted[37] heart,
>   With beams of mercy shine;
> And let thy healing voice impart
>   A taste of joys divine.
>
> Thy presence only can bestow
>   Delights which never cloy;[38]
> Be this my solace, here below,
>   And my eternal joy.

---

37. "Overtaken by the night." Johnson, *Dictionary of the English Language*, 20.

38. "To glut, surfeit, sate; to nail up." Johnson, *Dictionary of the English Language*, 35.

In a similar hymn, "Mourning the Absence of God, and Longing for His Gracious Presence,"[39] the speaker responds in other ways to a seemingly silent God. While the speaker appears to be facing the same circumstances as that of the previous hymn, her tone is much more desperate and forlorn in this latter one. Unlike most of the meters used in her other hymns, Steele uses the short meter (6.6.8.6) in this hymn, which Austin C. Lovelace refers to as the "exhorting meter, for its abrupt, direct opening line attracts attention."[40] The hymn begins with a rhetorical question, reflecting the speaker's anxiety about the absence of God, suggesting that she has been coping with His absence for a long time, so long that she has perhaps begun to doubt.

> My God, to thee I call—
> Must I forever mourn?
> So far from thee, my life, my all?
> O when wilt thou return?

The second verse is loaded with imagery of absolute darkness. Again, as in the previous hymn, the speaker appears to see herself as the root of the problem. It is her own "gloomy sorrows" that "hide [God's] soul-reviving light."[41] The same idea is expressed in the third verse with the line "my inward foes prevail"; the speaker is overtaken

---

39. Steele, *Poems on Subjects Chiefly Devotional & Miscellaneous Pieces*, Hymn 79, 141–42.

40. Austin C. Lovelace, *The Anatomy of Hymnody* (Chicago: G.I.A. Publications, 1965), 42.

According to Aalders, of the 105 hymns in *Poems on Subjects Chiefly Devotional*, Steele used common meter fifty-one times, long meter forty-eight times, and short meter five times. Aalders, *To Express the Ineffable*, 91.

41. Aalders observes of Steele's verse that she "most often located God in the celestial light of heaven while situating sinful humanity in darkness on earth. This distinction in location, which emphasizes the distance between God and people, between divine perfection and human sin, inability and incomprehension, reflects Steele's Calvinistic emphasis on God's transcendence…. This distance can be ascribed to the utter sinfulness of humanity." Aalders, *To Express the Ineffable*, 115.

by the inner psychological turmoil waging within her.[42] Her apprehension is evident by the conditional statement in the third verse; while it implies she knows that God is her only source of hope, she is nonetheless skeptical of whether He will provide her with it.

> Dark as the shades of night
> My gloomy sorrows rise,
> And hide thy soul-reviving light
> From these desiring eyes.

> My comforts all decay,
> My inward foes prevail;
> If thou withhold thy healing ray,
> Expiring hope will fail.

The fourth verse marks a change in tone. Even though the speaker feels alone in her suffering, she still has the confidence to command the "foes" within her to flee. While she may not feel the presence of God at the moment, she gives warning to them; her defense is that her God *is*, in fact, very near, that He *is* watching her, that He *does* acknowledge her every sigh. In other words, although the speaker *feels* abandoned in her suffering, deep down she knows she is not.

> Away, distressing fears,
> My gracious God is nigh,
> And heav'nly pity sees my tears,
> And marks each rising sigh.

Thus the speaker, turning from her "foes," moves to God and appeals to Him directly.

> Dear source of all my joys,
> And solace of my care,
> O wilt thou hear my plaintive voice
> And grant my humble pray'r!

---

42. Aalders states that the speaker's sorrow is what "draws a veil of cloud before God, resulting in troubling doubts which exacerbate her inability to understand the nature and ways of God." *To Express the Ineffable*, 128.

In the subsequent verse, the speaker is not hesitant in laying her doubts before God. She appeals to God to affirm her faith.

> These envious clouds remove,
>> Thy cheering light restore,
> Confirm my int'rest in thy love
>> Till I can doubt no more.

The final verse of the hymn shows that the speaker does not naively expect that God's "cheering light" will cause her troubles to vanish. She simply has faith that, should her suffering continue, God has the power to make her burden light.

> Then if my troubles rise,
>> To thee, my God, I'll flee,
> And raise my hopes above the skies,
>> And cast my cares on thee.

The Limitations of Earthly Solutions

Steele recognized that nothing in the world, no matter how appealing or gratifying, could satisfy her poor condition. She had tasted the sweetness of life's eases to the degree that the idea of parting with them triggered anxiety: "The dearest comforts of life are painfully sweet. O that I could enjoy them with thankfulness unmingled with anxious apprehensions of the pangs of separation!"[43] Just as she was aware of how easily one could be captivated by the world's charm, she was equally aware of its temporality, as seen in her hymn "God the Soul's Only Portion."[44]

> In vain the world's alluring smile
>> Would my unwary heart beguile:
> Deluding world! its brightest day,
>> Dream of a moment, fleets away!

---

43. Steele, *Miscellaneous Pieces in Verse and Prose by Theodosia*, included in Broome, *Bruised Reed*, 344.
44. Steele, *Poems on Subjects Chiefly Devotional & Miscellaneous Pieces*, Hymn 32, 80–81.

The poetic devices employed in the first verse reflect the message they communicate. The long meter (88.88) and rhyming couplets—with their neat symmetry and euphonic sounds—parallel the idea that the world possesses an "alluring smile" that "beguiles" the unsuspecting onlooker. We are immediately drawn into the plain and easy style of the hymn. Yet as the onlooker is captivated, just as quickly the onlooker is snapped out of it. Steele effectively uses the syntax of the final two lines of verse 1 to reflect its meaning. The second pair of couplets in verse 1 consists of pithy phrases and exclamatory expressions—the world's appeal is as short-lived as the very lines being read ("Deluding world!"; "Dream of a moment, fleets away!").

Describing the inadequacy of worldly pleasures, Steele uses vivid descriptions such as "pall," "languish," and "airy chaff." There is no questioning this verdict as Steele fills the imagination with words that convey distaste, decay, and waste.

> Earth's highest pleasures, could they last,
> Would pall and languish on the taste;
> Such airy chaff was ne'er design'd
> To feed th' immortal, craving mind.

The second couplet of the above verse is reminiscent of Psalm 1 where the wicked are likened to chaff that the wind blows away, in contrast to the "immortal, craving mind," which, delighting and meditating on God's Word, is likened to the tree planted by streams of water that lives, bears fruit, and prospers.

In verse 3, Steele refers to Lamentations 3:24, the scriptural verse that marks the title of the hymn: "The LORD is my portion, saith my soul; therefore will I hope in him." The hymn, of course, is not simply about the temporality of worldly pleasures, but about God being the only long-lasting hope.

> To nobler bliss my soul aspires,
> Come, Lord, and fill these vast desires;
> Be thou my portion, here I rest,
> Since of my utmost wish possest.

Having alluded to Scripture in the previous verses, it is no surprise that verse 4 pays tribute to the Word; it is what grants the speaker the assurance that she will not fall prey to the allurements of the world but cling to the Eternal. Divine love and heavenly hope reveal a bright world compared to the dark world the speaker inhabits.

> O let thy sacred word impart
> Its sealing influence to my heart;
> With pow'r, and light, and love divine,
> Assure my soul that thou art mine.
>
> The blissful word, with joy replete,
> Shall bid my gloomy fears retreat,
> And heav'n-born hope, serenely bright,
> Shine cheerful through this mortal night.

For the time being, the speaker holds onto this vision and relies on faith and the joy that the truths of the Word reveal to sustain her in this life.

> Then shall my joyful spirit rise
> On wings of faith above the skies;
> And when these transient scenes are o'er,
> And this vain world shall tempt no more:
>
> O may I reach the blissful plains,
> Where thy unclouded glory reigns,
> And dwell forever near thy throne
> In joys to mortal thought unknown.

In a hymn touching upon a similar theme, "Longing after Unseen Pleasures," Steele considers human reliance on worldly things to be the culprit for hindering her from seeing the grand purpose of God. Verses 3 and 4 discuss the transience of "earth's alluring toys":

> Their brightest day, alas, how vain!
>   With conscious sighs we own;
> While clouds of sorrow, care and pain,
>   O'ershade the smiling noon.

O could our thoughts and wishes fly,
    Above these gloomy shades,
To those bright worlds beyond the sky
    Which sorrow ne'er invades.[45]

Later in the hymn, in verse 5, the speaker indicates what is to be blamed: reason that offers insufficient insight into this life, satisfied with mere earthly happiness, and ignorance that knows not the fading properties of earthly victories.

There joys unseen by mortal eyes
    Or reason's feeble ray,
In ever-blooming prospect rise,
    Unconscious of decay.

Even more forceful is her expression of relief once these worldly things depart from her, evident in Steele's hymn "God My Only Happiness," particularly in the last two lines of verse 2:

When fill'd with grief, my anxious heart
    To thee, my God, complains,
Sweet pleasures mingles with the smart,[46]
    And softens all my pains.

Earth flies with all her soothing charms,
    Nor I the loss deplore;
No more, ye phantoms, mock my arms,
    Nor teaze my spirit more.[47]

---

45. Steele, *Poems on Subjects Chiefly Devotional & Miscellaneous Pieces,* Hymn 50, 103. This hymn will be discussed fully in chapter 4.

46. The feeling of "quick lively pain." Johnson, *Dictionary of the English Language,* 173.

47. Steele, *Poems on Subjects Chiefly Devotional & Miscellaneous Pieces,* Hymn 78, vv. 1–2, 140.

The comparison of the enticement of worldly things to the teasing of phantoms produces a foreboding image that gives caution to the unwary.[48]

In the above hymns, darkness overshadows the temporal world and serves to communicate the message that only when the speaker has released her grip on the things of the world can the presence of God be a light to her in her life.

Comfort from the Promises of the Word

In all these hymns that speak of the world's transience, what ought to be the anchor? In "God the Soul's Only Portion," the answer is the Word, which is full of God's bright promises: "O let thy sacred word impart/Its sealing influence to my heart.... The blissful word, with joy replete/Shall bid my gloomy fears retreat."[49] Why? Because God's promises cannot be frustrated by the passing of time or the changing of circumstances. Consider the third verse in "God My Only Happiness":

> I languish for superior joy
> To all that earth bestows;

---

48. "Phantoms" is a recurring image in Steele's poems, as in her poem "Happiness" (verse 9), in *Poems on Subjects Chiefly Devotional & Miscellaneous Pieces,* 184:

> Phantoms of pleasure rise, and smiling fair,
> They tempt our feet through labyrinths of care,
> Till catching at the prize we grasp the air.

The image also appears in her poem "A Meditation on Death," in *Poems on Subjects Chiefly Devotional & Miscellaneous Pieces,* 201:

> Come, bid adieu, my soul, to earthly pleasures—
> Illusive phantoms! distant how they smile,
> Fair as the colours of the radiant bow!
> But nearer fade upon the cheated eye,
> Lose all their lustre, or dissolve in air."

49. Steele, *Poems on Subjects Chiefly Devotional & Miscellaneous Pieces,* Hymn 32, vv. 4–5, 81.

> For pleasure which can never cloy,
> Nor change, nor period knows.[50]

The things of the world will inevitably fail to satisfy what the mortal most deeply needs. The speaker's "immortal mind" (Steele frequently applies this description to the human mind) longs, aspires, desires for more.[51] The promises of God offer true joy and bliss because only they are vast enough to fill her innermost needs, as she explains in verse 6.

> This joy, my wishes long to find,
> To his my heart aspires,
> A bliss, immortal as the mind,
> And vast as its desires!

The faithfulness of God finds its testimony in the Word. In one of Steele's most well-known hymns, "The Excellency of the Holy Scriptures," the character of God shines brightest in the Word:

---

50. Steele, *Poems on Subjects Chiefly Devotional & Miscellaneous Pieces,* Hymn 78, 140.

51. The following excerpts from Steele's poems, in *Poems on Subjects Chiefly Devotional & Miscellaneous Pieces,* 317, 258, and 325, show her belief that the mind was created to be satisfied by more:
In "The Complaint and Relief":
> Man has desires, capacious as his soul,
> Desires, which earthly joys can never fill.
> Can mortal food sustain the immortal mind?"

In "The Desire of Knowledge a Proof of Immortality":
> Surely, the mind must be akin to heaven;
> For heaven, all-wise, and infinitely good,
> Implants not these sublime desires in vain.
> If nought below immortal joys can fill
> The mind, the mind must be immortal too.

In "The Elevation":
> The restless mind, insatiate still,
> (Which all creation cannot fill,)
>> Fain would rise
>> Beyond the skies,
> And leave their glitt'ring wonders far behind.

> Father of mercies, in thy word
> What endless glory shines!
> For ever be thy name ador'd
> For these celestial lines.[52]

The hymn later shows in verse 6 the Word's power to penetrate the painful world of the sufferer. The flawed world is exposed for what it is as the sufferer wanders aimlessly through the untamed, deserted wilderness, dying of thirst, the forces of nature overwhelming her. In the same verses, however, Steele juxtaposes these awful conditions with equally liberating ones. The Word is a light that guides the lost. The phrase "beams of heaven" indicates just a *hint* of light amid the shadows, which the sufferer must then pursue in order to discern the right path.

> Amidst these gloomy wilds below,
> When dark and sad we stray;
> Here beams of heaven relieve our woe,
> And guide to endless day.

In the next verse, the Word is an invigorating spring that nourishes the fainthearted.

> Here springs of consolation rise,
> To cheer the fainting mind;
> And thirsty souls receive supplies,
> And sweet refreshment find.

Finally, the Word soothes the heart suffering from affliction.

> When guilt and terror, pain and grief,
> United rend the heart,
> Here sinners meet divine relief,
> And cool the raging smart.

---

52. Steele, *Poems on Subjects Chiefly Devotional & Miscellaneous Pieces*, Hymn 26, 72. Watson points out Steele's deliberate effort in this verse to produce the unexpected: "The endless glory is not heaven, but the word, the word on the page, and the celestial lines are not the lines of eternal life so much as the lines of Holy Scripture." Watson, *English Hymn*, 194.

These sensory images—of light, water, and coolness—convey the power of God's promises to provide comfort to the sufferer. The sufferer's eyes, once blinded by pain, have been opened by the Word.

Contemplation of the Character of God
Steele actively seeks to turn her thoughts to the person of God—His infiniteness, His perfections, His supreme rule—so that her aching, finite being might delight in a more promising state. In her hymn "Hope Encouraged in the Contemplation of the Divine Perfections," the speaker considers God's sovereignty over all creation, together with His goodness, which brings her to the sure conclusion that, while the future is unknown, she can trust Him in every circumstance. Verse 1 of the hymn comprises a series of questions that probe the character of God. According to Watson, in some of Steele's hymns, a question like this may be "unanswerable, and therein lies its point: God's ways and purposes are beyond our comprehension."[53] Thus in verse 1 the speaker describes the opposition between her human doubts and divine assurance. The speaker addresses her doubts by contemplating the character of God.

> Why sinks my weak desponding mind?
> Why heaves my heart the anxious sigh?
> Can sov'reign goodness be unkind?
> Am I not safe, if God is nigh?[54]

---

53. Watson, *English Hymn*, 192.
Aalders remarks, "One of the first things one notices when reading Steele's verse together is a certain lack of confident assertions. While she does, in keeping with other eighteenth-century hymn-writers, take care to pass along doctrine as she understands it—and as such, certain of her hymns have a decidedly didactic character—the form that her verse most often takes is that of questions and open-ended, probing verse." Aalders observes, accordingly, that Steele's hymns are often characterized by the question mark. Aalders, *To Express the Ineffable*, 124, 128.
54. Steele, *Poems on Subjects Chiefly Devotional & Miscellaneous Pieces*, Hymn 42, 93.

In verse 2, the speaker evokes God's sovereignty and goodness as well as His omniscience and omnipotence.

> He holds all nature in his hand:
> That gracious hand on which I live,
> Does life, and time, and death command,
> And has immortal joys to give.

In Steele's hymn "Complaining at the Throne of Grace," the initial five verses of the hymn describe the overwhelming suffering of the speaker; in addition, each of the verses reveals the progressive measures the speaker takes to seek God. In verse 1, the speaker approaches the throne of grace in utter anguish; in verse 2, though confronting silence, she does not protest; in verse 3, she acknowledges that God is the only true and trustworthy source; in verse 4, she resolves to entrust God with her suffering; and in verse 5, she appeals to God on the basis of His omniscience and omnipotence.

> O'erwhelm'd with restless griefs and fears,
> Lord, I approach thy mercy-seat,
> With aching heart and flowing tears,
> To pour my sorrows at thy feet.
>
> Can mournful penitence and pray'r
> Address thy mercy-seat in vain?
> Unnotic'd by thy gracious ear,
> Can sorrow and distress complain?
>
> Thy promises are large and free,
> To humble souls who seek thy face;
> O where for refuge can I flee,
> My God!—but to the throne of grace?
>
> My God, for yet my trembling heart
> Would fain[55] rely upon thy word;
> Fain would I bid my fears depart,
> And cast my burthen on the Lord.

---

55. "Glad, obliged, forced." Johnson, *Dictionary of the English Language*, 71.

> Thou see'st the tempest of my soul,
> These restless waves of fear and sin;
> Thy voice can all their rage control,
> And make a sacred calm within.[56]

In verse 6, the steps that the speaker has taken ultimately arouse her longing to see God.

> Amid the gloomy shades of night,
> To thee, I lift my longing eyes;
> My Saviour God, my life, my light,
> When will thy cheering beams arise?

The speaker conjures up comforting images of God by calling to mind His character as revealed in history. The remembrance is truly personal, evident in her utterance "my heart confess'd." The speaker's recalling of past moments of God's grace and deliverance in verse 7 is very real to her.

> My thoughts recall thy favours past,
> In many a dark distressing hour,
> Thy kind support my heart confess'd,
> And own'd thy wisdom, love, and pow'r.

Fond remembrances of God's dealings with her become a light during hardship. God's "unchanging faithfulness" (that is, His immutability) allows the speaker to trust Him even in the face of suffering.

> And still these bright perfections shine,
> Eternal their unclouded rays;
> Unchanging faithfulness is thine,
> And just, and right, are all thy ways.

A well-known hymn of Steele, "Humble Reliance," demonstrates the depth of her surrender to the sovereignty of God. Be it good health or longevity of life—should God deny her these blessings, her

---

56. Steele, *Poems on Subjects Chiefly Devotional & Miscellaneous Pieces*, Hymn 81, 144.

prayer is for a peaceful acceptance of whatever her lot would be.[57] In verse 3 of the hymn, the first three lines express the confidence of the speaker in the providence of God.

> Whate'er thy providence denies,
>   I calmly would resign,
> For thou art just, and good, and wise;
>   O bend my will to thine.[58]

The fourth line of this verse (separated from the first three by a semi-colon) shows that although the speaker may not be readily submissive, she asks God to bring her to a wholehearted submission to His will. The word "bend" implies the need for an external agent to intervene in order to produce transformation. Verse 4 is therefore a development of the idea expressed in verse 3; since wholehearted submission is not easy, the speaker asks God for strength to bear her load.

> Whate'er thy sacred will ordains,
>   O give me strength to bear;
> And let me know my Father reigns,
>   And trust his tender care.

The speaker's load, expressed in verses 5 and 6, includes the looming prospect of death. The speaker sees that God is no less merciful in such circumstances.

> If pain and sickness rend this frame,
>   And life almost depart,

---

57. "In a letter to Philip Furneaux, for example, Steele asserts that a 'sovereign hand' disperses 'Afflictive as well as smiling providences.' The personal ramifications of this belief are clarified in a letter to her brother, William Steele, where she writes, first, that she is 'yet in a poor state of health' and, then, that she desires 'to depend only on that sovereign Hand which dispenses Afflictions & Comforts in infinite Wisdom and Goodness.' And, given the preponderance of references to illness and death in Steele's letters and verse, this belief—that a sovereign God both allows and uses afflictions—is oft-repeated, even as it is repeated in the verse of other eighteenth-century writers." Aalders, *To Express the Ineffable*, 116.

58. Steele, *Poems on Subjects Chiefly Devotional & Miscellaneous Pieces*, Hymn 62, 118.

> Is not thy mercy still the same,
>   To cheer my drooping heart?
>
> If cares and sorrows me surround,
>   Their pow'r why should I fear?
> My inward peace they cannot wound,
>   If thou, my God, art near.

The speaker is honest about the weakness of her faith. Skepticism and disbelief naturally occupy the mind in times of suffering. In the process of contemplating the character of God, however, she is ultimately able to worship God and trust in His perfect will.

> Thy sov'reign ways are all unknown
>   To my weak, erring sight;
> Yet let my soul, adoring, own
>   That all thy ways are right.
>
> My God, my Father, be thy name
>   My solace and my stay;
> O wilt thou seal my humble claim,
>   And drive my fears away.

Furthermore, Steele's prose reveals that her understanding and trust in the character of God enabled her to see that suffering could be a form of loving discipline:

> Even this affliction, may I not call it a blessing from the happy effects which I hope it has produced? May I not esteem it a paternal correction to reprove my ungrateful coldness, to awaken me to a state of sensibility, and renew the relish of those important blessings which have been almost neglected, or at best too faintly sought? How gentle, O my God, were the strokes of thy chastising hand.[59]

In humility, Steele learned to recognize what her suffering had produced in her. When enjoying more privileged circumstances, she confessed that she had grown cold and insensitive to the divine

---

59. Steele, *Miscellaneous Pieces in Verse and Prose by Theodosia*, in Broome, *Bruised Reed*, 344.

blessings in her life. However, God used her affliction to mold her character. With her spirit of gratitude kindled, Steele realized that her affliction could even be considered a "gentle stroke" in light of what she ultimately gained from it.[60]

Jesus Christ—The Only True Comfort

For Steele, her physical condition was not nearly as critical as her spiritual one. This truth is illustrated in the ensuing two hymns—the first one relating to sickness, the second one to death. In the first verse of the hymn "The Great Physician," sin is depicted as the real sickness, the source of the sinner's pain.

> Ye mourning sinners, here disclose
> Your deep complaints, your various woes;
> Approach, 'tis Jesus, he can heal
> The pains which mourning sinners feel.[61]

The hymn is based on Luke 6:19, which describes a crowd gathering around Jesus, eager to be healed of their diseases: "And the whole multitude sought to touch him: for there went virtue out of

---

60. Consider also Steele's letter written in response to Caleb Ashworth (principal of a Nonconformist Academy and friend of Steele). Ashworth had visited Steele in Broughton and, while he expressed admiration for her writing, he also expressed his concern about "some expressions" of her "dropt of doubt." She responded: "I hope I have reason to bless God for the sweet consolations I have sometimes enjoyed in seasons of affliction, that all the dispensations of providence are not only just and wise but good and kind…. The thoughts which occasioned those expressions of doubt which you observed, frequently occur, but also frequently lead me to examine the foundation of the evidences of my hope; and think [if I am not deceived] it is generally more confirmed by the trial. I hope I can sometimes experience the happy effects that you mention of renewed application to the precious blood of Jesus and desires for the sanctifying comforting influences of his Spirit. O may I ever keep in view my own weakness, my utter unworthiness and the perfect righteousness and all sufficiency of grace of the Great Redeemer!" Anne Steele to Caleb Ashworth (September 9, 1763), STE 2/13/ix, Angus Library, Regent's Park College, Oxford; quoted in Broome, *Bruised Reed*, 182–83.

61. Steele, *Poems on Subjects Chiefly Devotional & Miscellaneous Pieces*, Hymn 5, 36.

him, and healed them all." In verses 3 to 6, however, leprosy, fever, and palsy are used to portray the sickness of the soul and mind. Leprosy, a vile disease that disfigures the skin, is compared to sin that infects the soul in verse 4.

> Nor shall the leper, hopeless lie
> Beneath the Great Physician's eye;
> Sin's deepest pow'r his word controuls,
> That fatal leprosy of souls.

Fever, a symptom that renders the body pale and feeble, able to plunge its victim into uncontrollable fits, is compared to the tempestuous mind that is "burning" and "restless" for peace in verse 5.[62]

> That hand divine, which can assuage
> The burning fever's restless rage;
> That hand, omnipotent and kind,
> Can cool the fever of the mind.

In verse 6, palsy, paralysis that leaves the body "frozen," motionless, is compared to the invasive and irrepressible reality of death.

> When freezing palsy chills the veins,
> And pale, cold death, already reigns,
> He speaks; the vital pow'rs revive:
> He speaks, and dying sinners live.

The crucial message of Jesus, which underlies this hymn, is that the true need of the sick is the Great Physician Himself. Hence, in the second couplet of the above verse, "He speaks" is repeated—the first time the "vitals" are revived; the second time (anticipated by

---

62. In Steele's hymn "Christ the Physician of Souls" in *Poems on Subjects Chiefly Devotional & Miscellaneous Pieces*, Hymn 28, v. 2, 76, sin is also likened to fever. Steele would have suffered from recurring episodes of fever as a result of her malaria, which makes the comparison all the more personal.

> Sin like a raging fever reigns,
> With fatal strength in ev'ry part;
> The dire contagion fills the veins,
> And spreads its poison to the heart.

the colon in the previous line) "dying sinners" are given life. In Luke 6:20–23, Jesus preaches the Beatitudes, which begin, "Blessed be ye poor: for yours is the kingdom of God." It is the sick who are made to see that they cannot save themselves but that they need the healing power of Jesus. The images in the above verses furthermore demonstrate the power of Jesus to heal *instantly*—it is Jesus' "word" that controls, His "hand" that assuages and cools, His lips that "speak" and revive. The idea that the dying sinner can be healed immediately upon faith culminates in verse 7 below.

> Dear Lord, we wait thy healing hand;
> Diseases fly at thy command:
> O let thy sov'reign touch impart
> Life, strength, and health to ev'ry heart!

The final verse illustrates the natural impulse of the healed to make their healing known.

> Then shall the sick, the blind, the lame,
> Adore their Great Physician's name;
> Then dying souls shall bless their God,
> And spread thy wond'rous praise abroad.

In Steele's hymn "An Evening Reflection,"[63] the speaker envisions her death. The words to the hymn are so deeply personal that we can picture Steele lying in bed, in the solitude of the dark, still night, brooding about her own mortality.

> Another day is past,
>   The hours for ever fled,
> And time is bearing me in haste,
>   To mingle with the dead.
>
> Perhaps my closing eyes
>   No more may hail the light,
> Seal'd up, before the morning rise,
>   In everlasting night.

---

63. Steele, *Poems on Subjects Chiefly Devotional & Miscellaneous Pieces,* Hymn 25, 70–72.

Reflecting on the prospect of her own death, the speaker realizes that her role in this life is not a passive one. Knowing that death does not signal the end of life but the beginning of another, she must ready herself. The task is pressing as the soul is described as being on the "brink of vast eternity." We are just *one* moment away from where we are to be eternally.

> But I've a part to live,
>   A never dying ray,
> The soul, immortal, will survive
>   The ruins of her clay.
>
> This mortal frame must lie
>   Unconscious in the tomb,
> But oh! Where will my spirit fly,
>   And what will be her doom?
>
> On the tremendous brink
>   Of vast eternity,
> Where souls with strange amazement shrink,
>   What will my prospect be?

The gravity of the speaker's situation is intensified by the depiction of hell and the speaker's trepidation.

> When the dark gulph below,
>   With death and horror fraught,
> Reveals its scenes of endless woe—
>   Oh dreadful, dreadful thought!

What liberates her from this horrific image is Jesus, for *His* death on the cross has defeated death and eternal judgment. Steele continues in the hymn by reflecting on this victory.

> But lo! yon shining skies
>   Beam down a cheerful ray,
> And bid my drooping hopes arise
>   To glorious realms of day.
>
> 'Tis there my Saviour lives,
>   My Lord, my life, my light;

His blissful name my soul revives—
  Adieu to death and night.

He conquer'd death and hell,
  And his victorious love
Shall bear his ransom'd friends, to dwell
  In his bright courts above.

Jesus! and art thou mine?
  O let thy heav'nly voice
Confirm my hope with pow'r divine,
  And bid my soul rejoice.

The hymn concludes with the speaker's calm resignation to the inevitability and even imminence of her death, expressed simply yet beautifully.

Then shall my closing eyes,
  Contented, sink to rest;
For if to night this body dies,
  My spirit shall be blest.

In the above hymns, the speaker—confronted with sickness and death, and even more importantly, confronted with her own sin—is reassured by her intimate knowledge of Jesus.[64] In Steele's hymn "Sin the Cause of Sorrow," the speaker's knowledge becomes a profound comfort during moments when she feels the inaccessibility of God.

Yes, I have cause indeed to mourn,
  When God conceals his radiant face;
And pray and long till he return,
  With smiles of sweet forgiving grace.

Then weep my eyes, complain my heart,
  But mourn not, hopeless of relief;
For sov'reign mercy will impart
  Its healing beams, to ease my grief.

---

64. Broome observes of Steele's theology, "Besides a deep knowledge of Christ Anne had that deep knowledge of sin, which must precede it. This is made clear in many of her hymns." Broome, *Bruised Reed*, 170.

The speaker then shines the spotlight on her Savior. She knows that to seek God is to call on Him in the name of Christ. The hymn concludes with an image of the sacrifice of the Son.

> The Saviour pleads his dying blood,
>   Awake my hope, away my fears;
> Through him I'll seek my absent God,
>   Till his returning smile appears.[65]

Encountering God's absence, the speaker has appealed to Christ, the revelation of the Father who cannot be seen.

Finally, in Steele's hymn "Searching after Happiness," the speaker is able to glory in her afflictions because of her vision of the end of the journey.[66] According to Aalders, the metaphor of life as a journey frequently surfaces in Steele's writing:

> Steele often writes of life as a journey—a journey on which she suffered many disappointing delays and painful detours. She travels this journey "in a frail, shatter'd bark," language which brings to mind the fragile body in which she moved through life. Life, for Steele, is a "toilsome journey"; more than this, it is a "disastrous journey" marked by "pain and grief." Elsewhere, Steele judges life to be "a mazy Wild" in which "We pant, and

---

65. Steele, *Poems on Subjects Chiefly Devotional & Miscellaneous Pieces*, Hymn 36, vv. 3–5, 86–87.

66. In her poem "Submission to God under Affliction, and Desiring Support," in *Poems on Subjects Chiefly Devotional & Miscellaneous Pieces*, 272, Steele writes about how prone the soul is to forget about the end of the journey:

> O let my soul the wond'rous pow'r confess
> Of sov'reign mercy, and adore the hand,
> Whose just rebukes, with kind indulgence mix'd,
> Are meant to teach, reclaim, and guide my feet,
> Too apt to rove, forgetful of the way,
> Forgetful of the end. A crown of life,
> Of life immortal, is the glorious prize,
> (Free gift of boundless grace!) which in the view
> Of faith and humble love thy word displays;
> Obtain'd by suff'rings which amaz'd the world.

toil, and wish in vain for rest"; but rest is not found in "this dark Wilderness, this vale of tears."[67]

In the verses below, however, the journeyer finds reprieve.

> There Jesus, source of bliss divine,
>   Our glorious leader reigns;
> He gives us strength to hold our way,
>   And crowns the traveller's pains.
>
> Dear Saviour, let thy cheering smile
>   My fainting soul renew;
> Then shall the heav'nly Canaan yield
>   A sweet, though distant view.
>
> Be thy almighty arm my stay,
>   My guide through all the road,
> Till safe I reach my journey's end,
>   My Saviour, and my God.[68]

With Christ, suffering is not an end in itself but rather a symbol of the cross, and so the speaker carries it with hope, joy, and honor. The speaker is able to carry her load because she knows that Christ, her "glorious leader," suffered for her. As wearying as the journey may be, she faithfully and obediently wears the crown. Because of Christ, the land of rest is in sight.

Conclusion

The hymns examined in this chapter show that Steele's vision enabled her to submit willingly to God, even in the face of suffering. Her vision was of a loving God who had sovereign control over her circumstances. At the same time, however, Steele was honest about the moments when she needed the grace of God to strengthen her faith. In her moments of human weakness, her suffering had affected her desire to worship God wholeheartedly and

---

67. Aalders, *To Express the Ineffable*, 109.
68. Steele, *Poems on Subjects Chiefly Devotional & Miscellaneous Pieces*, Hymn 11, vv. 7–9, 46.

made her despair when she did not feel the comfort of God's presence. Rather than resorting to worldly comfort, however, Steele resolutely turned to God. She sought God through His Word, through remembrances of how He had delivered her in the past, and above all through Christ. Steele's spiritual vision was therefore built on a solid foundation. As we shall see in the next chapter, it was this foundation that enabled her to sustain a strong vision of the heavenly glory.

Time is but a point,
and mortal pains or joys are light as air,
when vast eternity is full in view.

CHAPTER FOUR

Hope in the Promised Glory

"Nothing is more certain than death, as all experience in all ages testify; and yet nothing more uncertain than the time…. No man has power over his spirit, to retain the spirit one moment, when it is called for," wrote John Gill.[1] Living in a world subject to decay and corruption, God's people are offered tremendous hope in the heavenly glory that is revealed in Scripture. There will be a day when such despairing realities will no longer have dominion over the earth (Rom. 8:19–21). While death is "formidable" to nature, it is "desirable" for believers, for to be absent from the body is to be present with the Lord.[2]

Sustaining hope in the heavenly glory requires a laboring and striving because of the obstacles that lie in the way of believers:

> Things hoped for are difficult to come at and possess; many tribulations lie in the way to the kingdom, through which men must enter into it; the righteous, by reason of many afflictions, trials, and temptations, are *scarcely saved*, though at last certainly saved; and since the *gate is strait and the way narrow*, which lead to eternal life; hence there must be a labouring and striving to enter in; of which there is hope: and therefore, hope is of things possible, or otherwise it would turn to despair.[3]

---

1. Gill, *Body of Practical and Doctrinal Divinity*, 405–6.
2. Gill, *Body of Practical and Doctrinal Divinity*, 406.
3. Gill, *Body of Practical Divinity*, 755.

What saves believers from this despair is God's own promise. In the midst of glories unseen, it is His promise onto which believers cling: "The glories of another world are things not seen, so as thoroughly to understand and comprehend, yet hope of enjoying them, upon the divine promise, is conversant with them" (Rom. 8:24–25; Heb. 6:19).[4]

Above all, the object of hope for God's people is salvation offered by Jesus Christ; through Him they are pardoned of sin and receive all blessings of grace in this life and hereafter (Ps. 130:7).[5] Eternal life is thus the "grand object of hope" (Titus 1:2; 2:13; Rom. 5:2; Col. 1:5); it is a free gift, owed entirely to the free grace of God.[6] God's people are to ready themselves for this day, praying and remembering that Jesus has gone to prepare heaven and happiness for them "by his presence and mediation; and has promised to come again and take them to himself, that they may be with him, where he is; and for this he prays and makes intercession" (John 14:2–3; 17:24).[7]

It is hope in the promised glory then that weans God's people from the world since they know that they have a more lasting aim. Seeking the things that lie beyond this world, they have the hope of rejoicing in the glory of God. It is this hope that carries them through the hardships of life, making hard things easy: "Hope of a future state of happiness beyond the grave, bears them up under all the troubles of the present state, and carries them comfortably through them, so that they glory in tribulation" (Rom. 5:3–5).[8] It is this hope that shines a light in life's darkest moment: "It yields support in death; for *the righteous hath hope in his death* (Prov. 14:32), not founded on his own righteousness, but on the righteousness of Christ; a hope of being with Christ for ever, and of enjoying eternal life and happiness with him; and which gives him peace and joy in

---

4. Gill, *Body of Practical Divinity*, 755.
5. Gill, *Body of Practical Divinity*, 755.
6. Gill, *Body of Practical Divinity*, 757.
7. Gill, *Body of Practical Divinity*, 758.
8. Gill, *Body of Practical Divinity*, 760.

his last moments, and causes him to exult in the view of death and the grave."[9]

In our complacency, the earth shines in all its beauty; in our sorrow, heaven in all its glory. Perhaps heaven becomes the greatest comfort when a person is forced to face his or her own mortality. This was certainly true for Steele toward the end of her life, as we shall see.

The Final Years

Steele's preparation of the third and final volume of her manuscript took place during her last years. This was "a time in which she was confined to bed and in very poor health, and it is likely that death would have figured prominently in her thoughts during this time."[10] As Steele began to close the curtain on her literary efforts, she must have "contemplated her imminent death and the completion of the literary task she had accepted from God."[11] Steele's poems, especially those relating to the subject of death, reveal the sort of thoughts that passed through the writer's mind when she was facing this difficult period in her life. Responding to the death of a relative, for instance, she wrote:

> While grief supplies the unavailing tear,
> Reflection points our own approaching end.
> That end approaching is our chief concern,
> Life's most important business is, to die.[12]

Steele's writing shows that she sympathized with humanity and its natural instinct to avoid reflecting on the "awful gloom" of death: "Fear spreads, to hide the distant scene."[13] Death conjures vexing thoughts that terrorize the soul, preventing it from moving beyond the gloom:

---

9. Gill, *Body of Practical Divinity*, 760.

10. Aalders, *To Express the Ineffable*, 132.

11. Aalders, *To Express the Ineffable*, 132, 134.

12. Anne Steele, "On Receiving a Mourning Ring for a Young Relative," *Miscellaneous Pieces, in Verse and Prose, by Theodosia*, 38.

13. Steele, "A Thought of Life and Death," *Miscellaneous Pieces, in Verse and Prose, by Theodosia*, 69.

> The parting pangs I fear,
> Alarm this timorous, fainting heart,
>   And still it lingers here.[14]

But facing the reality of death was critical to Steele. The theme is also addressed in the earlier volumes of her manuscript. Steele believed it was necessary to make herself *conscious* of this reality—to not close her eyes on it as if in a "careless slumber," but to let the reality affect her in order that "important truths" emerge. While death no doubt triggers "awful" thoughts, it serves as a "warning," an "admonition," a "striking form" that is meant to give her "better thoughts."

> Awake, my soul,
> Nor, careless, slumber on the brink of fate.
> With constant warnings, with loud admonitions,
> Can I be unconcern'd? At length my eyes,
> Long held in mists, or cheated with false visions,
> Begin to open on the awful scene.
> Let idle-active fancy, now no more
> Spread her gay, flatt'ring colours to my view;
> But aid my better thoughts, and represent
> Important truths in all their striking forms.[15]

And so, wherever Steele looked, however ordinary the circumstances, she saw the world through this lens. Chapter 2 showed that Steele knew to enjoy and appreciate the beauty of creation, but her observations of the changes in its landscape were reminders of what that beauty pointed to: its inevitable demise. The withering flower, the dying bush—these were merely mirrors of the natural course her own life would take.

> See yonder stalk! there lately grew a flow'r,
> 'Tis gone, its glowing colours are no more.
> That bush, where roses smil'd, and breath'd perfume!

14. Steele, "A Thought of Life and Death," *Miscellaneous Pieces, in Verse and Prose, by Theodosia*, 69.

15. Steele, "A Meditation on Death," *Poems on Subjects Chiefly Devotional & Miscellaneous Pieces*, 201.

How sweet their fragrance, and how gay their bloom!
A few days since they bloom'd, now dropt and lost:
Frail mortal life, behold how vain thy boast!
…My last will come, and this may be the day.
Each pain I feel, and every plaintive sigh,
What does it speak? this truth—"I soon must die."[16]

Preparing her final volume while battling sickness, Steele had to confront this reality and ask the fundamental question concerning the state of her own soul.

Oppress'd with pain my feeble powers decay,
The springs of life wear out, the vital flame
Seems quivering near its exit. Is the day
At hand which shall dissolve this mortal frame?

If this frail tottering mansion soon should fall,
Art thou, my soul, prepar'd to take thy flight?
Prepar'd, at thy almighty Father's call,
To quit, with joy, the scenes of mortal night?[17]

The soul and its condition were in the forefront of Steele's consciousness; thus she knew to commit her time, her energies, and her life to God.

O be that life, which thy indulgent hand
Sustain'd when sinking to the shades of death,
Devoted to thy praise, whose kind command
Restores my wasting strength and shortening breath.
Be my remaining hours entirely thine,
My strength and breath employ'd in work divine.[18]

---

16. Steele, "The Death Watch," *Poems on Subjects Chiefly Devotional & Miscellaneous Pieces*, 215–16.

17. Steele, "Written in a Painful Illness," *Miscellaneous Pieces, in Verse and Prose, by Theodosia*, 55.

18. Steele, "On Recovery from Sickness," *Miscellaneous Pieces, in Verse and Prose, by Theodosia*, 84.

Grappling with fears and enduring great pain, Steele persisted in focusing her thoughts on the end. These thoughts, while not unbroken, gave her the strength she deeply needed to face it.

> When now and then a heavenly ray
>   Attracts my upward view,
> Almost I hail the approach of day,
>   And bid the world adieu.[19]

Steele must have longed for her pain to be over. In one of the poems in her earlier volumes, she writes about her hunger to see the journey's end:

> —'Tis but to wait with patience
> A few sad hours, a few more painful steps,
> And life's fatiguing pilgrimage is o'er.
> Soon will my weary eyelids close in death,
> And these poor feeble limbs sink down to rest
> In the cold bosom of the silent grave.[20]

These excerpts from Steele's poetry help us grasp how she was able to meet the challenges that were ahead of her. At one time, she wrote to her half-sister, Mary, describing her situation: "The declining year, as well as my weak state of body, reminds me that all things are tending to their dissolution."[21]

Between 1770 and 1778, Steele's health deteriorated significantly. On top of suffering from irritable bowel syndrome and peptic ulceration of the stomach, she endured excruciatingly painful toothaches. Her malaria made her anemic and vulnerable to perpetual infection. By June 17, 1771, Steele was so gravely ill that

---

19. Steele, "A Thought of Life and Death," *Miscellaneous Pieces, in Verse and Prose, by Theodosia*, 69.

20. Steele, "The Pilgrim," *Poems on Subjects Chiefly Devotional & Miscellaneous Pieces*, 277.

21. Anne Steele to Mary Steele Wakeford (n.d.), STE 3/10 (vi), Angus Library, Regent's Park College, Oxford; quoted in Aalders, *To Express the Ineffable*, 150.

she was confined to her bed for much of the time until her death at the age of sixty-one on November 11, 1778.

While those final years showed slight improvements in her condition, they were only momentary. In 1772, she experienced trembling and shaking, or what was described as "fits," which was likely a result of her malaria. In 1777, she also began to suffer from deafness.[22] Her niece Polly (that is, Mary Steele, daughter of William Steele Jr. and his first wife, Mary [née Bullock, 1753–1813]), who was the primary caregiver of Steele during her sickness, noted that her aunt's final days consisted of few "lucid moments," an indication perhaps that she endured some form of dementia or semiconsciousness.[23]

From 1770 onward, having to cope with years of acute suffering, Steele left an indelible mark on the family and friends around her. Jane Attwater (1753–1844), Steele's cousin,[24] was by her side in her final days. Jane kept a diary that records intimate details about Steele's condition, revealing the depth of her spirituality, even at the very end of her life.[25]

A week before Steele's death, Jane visited her cousin in Broughton and described her poor physical condition. It was clear that Steele was soon to pass on into eternity, for she looked frail and could barely speak. Jane shared in her diary, however, that just

---

22. Broome, *Bruised Reed,* 203–4.

23. Broome, *Bruised Reed,* 214–15. Steele and Polly had a close relationship, since Steele had been a "surrogate mother to [Polly] from the time of the death of her mother in 1762 until her father remarried in 1768." Polly devoted nine years of her life caring for her aunt in her own home at Broughton House. Broome, *Bruised Reed,* 200–201.

24. Jane was Steele's second cousin, daughter of Steele's stepmother's niece (of the Cator family). The two were longtime companions; Jane frequently visited Steele in Broughton. Broome, *Bruised Reed*, 129.

25. For more information, see Marjorie Reeves, "Jane Attwater's Diaries," in *Pilgrim Pathways: Essays in Baptist History in Honour of B. R. White*, ed. William H. Brackney, Paul S. Fiddes, and John H. Y. Briggs (Macon, Ga.: Mercer University Press, 1999), 207–22. See also Marjorie Reeves, *Sheep Bell and Ploughshare: The Story of Two Village Families* (Bradford-on-Avon: Moonraker Press, 1978).

before leaving her side, Steele had taken her hand and in loving-kindness said, "Farewell till we meet in a happier world."[26] Jane left her side in tears, believing that she would never see her dear cousin again this side of eternity.[27] The day after Steele's death, Jane's diary entry states that her final moments prior to departing were "without a murmur and almost without a sigh." While Steele undoubtedly suffered tremendous physical pain, Jane wrote that "her future prospect administered consolation to her soul."

Writing about Steele's funeral, Jane records that Pastor Josiah Lewis of Broughton Church had preached from John 14:2–3, a passage chosen by Steele years prior specifically for her own funeral.[28] Lewis comforted the mourning family and friends at the funeral by reminding them of Steele's own hopeful outlook regarding her death:

> In my Father's house are many mansions: if it were not so, I would have told you. I go to prepare a place for you. And if I go

26. Diary of Jane Attwater (November 4, 1778), Late Dr. Marjorie Reeves's Collection, Angus Library, Regent's Park College, Oxford; quoted in Broome, *Bruised Reed*, 216.

27. It is worth noting that in the same diary entry, Jane mentions the presence of Samuel Stennett (1727–1795) and Caleb Evans, both leading London Particular Baptist ministers. The fact that these men had journeyed from London and Bristol to see Steele shows the importance she had in the Calvinistic Baptist community. Broome, *Bruised Reed*, 216. In fact, in the preface to the 1780 edition of Steele's hymns, Evans described the moments leading up to Steele's death: "Having been confined to her chamber some years before her death, she had long waited with Christian dignity for the awful hour of her departure. She often spoke, not merely with tranquility, but joy of her decease."

28. Broome, *Bruised Reed*, 217. Josiah Lewis was ordained there as pastor on October 14, 1778, shortly after the resignation of Pastor Nathaniel Rawlings on November 21, 1777. Broome, *Bruised Reed*, 214.

Regarding the spirit and character of Attwater's diaries, Reeves writes, "One could conclude from the diaries alone that her chief concern in life was attending religious meetings. She was certainly an addicted sermoniser, with an appetite for three every Sunday, with any available weekday religious gatherings thrown in. Her memory must have been prodigious, for her sermon outlines often cover several pages in the diary." Reeves, "Jane Attwater's Diaries," 208.

and prepare a place for you, I will come again, and receive you unto myself; that where I am, there ye may be also.

Although Lewis may not have had the opportunity to be well acquainted with Steele, as she had passed away four weeks after he had taken on the pastorate at Broughton Church, during his sermon he revealed the following regarding her spirituality:

> Our friend herself, I am informed, warmly requested that nothing of the kind [that is, sorrow without hope] might be spoken upon this occasion.... You can look back with pleasure upon those many hours of free conversation you formerly had with her, (and I mean particularly on religious matters) for which some of you have told me she had a distinguished talent, and you are willing, I persuade myself, to acknowledge the benefit you received thereby.[29]

It was evident that many told the pastor about their fondness for Steele, for in his sermon Lewis brought to attention the various heartfelt words Steele uttered on her deathbed, which lay bare the many different but honest faces of an individual who was enduring great pain and facing her own mortality: "The few last hours our friend had on earth, so far as spectators could judge, appeared to be more than ordinarily painful. At one time she said, 'It is hard work,' and at another, that 'she endured unspeakable pain,' that 'She knew that her Redeemer lived,' and at another to a friend that stood by, 'She entreated her to pray that her faith might not fail.'"[30]

Lewis also pointed out Steele's willingness to surrender to her sovereign God, even in her pain: "Frequently did she acknowledge the righteousness of the divine procedure and that it was her duty and her wish to submit to whatever God was pleased to lay upon her." Describing the final seconds of her death, Lewis said, "She sunk gradually under the decays of nature, and at the instant she expired [which was without a sigh or groan], she raised up her hand to a considerable height, in the full enjoyment of reason, and gently waved it, an

29. Broome, *Bruised Reed,* 217.
30. Broome, *Bruised Reed,* 218.

expression it was supposed by those who were near that all was well and that she was done with time, that angels were at hand and she was going to one of those mansions prepared for her in the world above."[31]

In the conclusion of his sermon, Lewis painted a vivid portrait of Steele's spirituality:

> What an honour does such a death as hers, reflect upon the religion of Jesus…. What a striking evidence is it of the truth of that religion…. Such a comfortable frame is methinks one of the noblest sights our eyes can behold. Now she has put off her sackcloth and is girded with gladness; and long before now, it has been echoed throughout the heavenly plains, here is one who is come out of great tribulation, who has washed her robes and made them white in the blood of the Lamb.[32]

Steele's final words prior to her death from Job 19:25 are well known: "I know that my Redeemer liveth." Upon witnessing her final journey—her last utterances, her preparation for her own death, her peaceful acceptance of her condition and her mortality—we can see that her dying words were a genuine representation of what she believed. Christ was her hope; in Him there was no sorrow in death for, to Steele, death was not the end.

The Promised Glory

Authentic Faith

In Steele's hymn "Faith in the Joys of Heaven,"[33] based on 2 Corinthians 5:7, "For we walk by faith, not by sight," the speaker questions the veracity of her own faith. She begins with a plain truth in the first verse: faith brings believers a joy that derives from heaven, not earth. If this is indeed the truth, however, why is it that the speaker is unable to look to the things above? What is the substance of her faith? Why the heavy reliance on the bodily senses and the hesitation to rely on faith?

---

31. Broome, *Bruised Reed,* 218.

32. Broome, *Bruised Reed,* 218.

33. Steele, *Poems on Subjects Chiefly Devotional & Miscellaneous Pieces,* Hymn 33, 82–83.

Faith leads to joys beyond the sky;
   Why then is this weak mind
Afraid to raise a cheerful eye
   To more than sense can find?

Verse 2 elaborates on the futility of relying on the senses. The human sensory organs are limited: they can process only what is filtered through the earthly body and hence can perceive only the things belonging to the earthly realm.[34] To rely solely on the sensory organs, then, is to overlook what the sensory organs are unable to discern—the things belonging to the heavenly realm.

Sense can but furnish scenes of woe,
   In this low vale of tears;
No groves of heav'nly pleasures grow,
   No paradise appears.

Verse 3 challenges the human instinct to rely on the senses. When it comes to relying on the world to find happiness, experience proves that sooner or later such ambitions will be foiled by the world's limitations. The speaker therefore wonders why she still persists in such a state of restlessness.[35] By presenting this reality in

---

34. Steele expresses this reality in stark terms in her poem "True Pleasure in Divine Meditation," in *Poems on Subjects Chiefly Devotional & Miscellaneous Pieces*, 293–94:

Come, sacred contemplation, heavenly guest,
And bring the muse to bless the lonely hour.
Unbind my fetter'd thoughts, and bid them rise
Above these low, dull, tiresome, empty scenes,
To nobler objects; spread the mental feast,
A rich variety. The heaven-born mind
Should never meanly stoop to feed on trash,
Nor mingle with the appetites of sense.

35. The idea that relying on the bodily senses leads to human restlessness is similarly expressed in Steele's poem "The Desire of Knowledge a Proof of Immortality," in *Poems on Subjects Chiefly Devotional & Miscellaneous Pieces*, 258:

the form of rhetorical questions, Steele effectively exposes the utter senselessness in it.

> Ah! Why should this mistaken mind
>   Stil' rove with restless pain?
> Delight on earth expect to find,
>   Yet still expect in vain?

This is why faith is the answer to human restlessness, not the senses. Even Eden (earth's paradise) in all its splendor pales in comparison to heaven in all its glory. Faith is personified in verse 4 below because it occupies a central role; faith ultimately awards its possessor a far more promising perspective.[36]

> Faith, rising upward, points her view
>   To regions in the skies;
> There lovelier scenes than Eden knew,
>   In bright perspective rise.

Verse 5 opens with a compelling statement: the speaker questions the state of her own faith. If her faith were indeed authentic, would not her thoughts be directed toward heaven? Again, by

> What is this thinking pow'r, this active mind,
> Which nought on earth can satiate, nought can bound?
> Restless it roams the wide creation o'er
> In search of something more than sense can give.
> Whate'er delights, the senses must decline;
> 'Tis short-liv'd pleasure, momentary joy.
> The senses soon are tir'd, and sink to rest.

36. The role of faith is similarly described in the following poem "The Prospect," in *Poems on Subjects Chiefly Devotional & Miscellaneous Pieces*, 244:

> O for a beam of glory from above,
> To bid the intervening clouds remove;
> From earth's low dregs to purge the visual ray,
> And clear my prospect to the realms of day.
> Dim is the eye of sense; but faith supplies
> (Inspir'd by heaven) what feeble sense denies.
> In revelation's glass, celestial aid,
> Applied by faith, what wonders are display'd!

presenting this reality in the form of a rhetorical question, Steele calls attention to the fact that there is no other alternative. Authentic faith ought to manifest thoughts of future glory.

> Oh! If this heav'n-born grace were mine,
> 　Would not my spirit soar,
> Transported gaze on joys divine,
> 　And cleave to earth no more?

In verse 6, the speaker indicts herself. The bright rays of heaven have not yet penetrated her human senses. The speaker tries, but earthly doubts, fears, and vanities have compromised her faith. While the speaker is not faithless, her faith is nonetheless described as "weak" and dying away. The exclamatory statement and short successive phrases convey a feeling of urgency—if the speaker does not do something soon, the glories of heaven will elude her.

> If in my heart true faith appears,
> 　How weak the sacred ray!
> Feebly aspiring, prest with fears,
> 　Almost it dies away.

The speaker knows that it is not by her own power that her faith will be strengthened but by God's power. She therefore summons God, the one who first infused faith in her, to inspire her faith to reach for the joys that are beyond this earthly life. The human body, with its limitations, is the culprit and the reason her vision is clouded. The meaninglessness of worldly living weighs down on her body. But with the brilliance of heaven lighting the way, the speaker trusts that her eyes will be opened.[37] The hymn concludes with a hopeful out-

---

37. In the following poem "The Elevation," in *Poems on Subjects Chiefly Devotional & Miscellaneous Pieces*, 325–26, not only are the senses limited, but also "proud science," "bold philosophy," and creation alone. It is faith, relying on the "sacred Word," that fills the "longing mind" and leads to life.

> Wonders, all to sense unknown!
> Glories, seen by faith alone!
> Come, faith, with heaven-illumin'd ray,
> Arise, and lead the shining way,

look. The speaker, no longer driven by her "weak, erring" senses but by spiritual passion, will at last ascend to heavenly heights.

> O thou, from whose almighty breath
>> It first began to rise,
> Purge off these mists, these dregs of earth,
>> And bid it reach the skies.
>
> Let this weak, erring mind no more,
>> On earth bewilder'd rove,
> But with celestial ardour soar
>> To endless joys above.

The Blinding Effect of Sin

The previous hymn is a good bridge to the next one, which makes clear the reason our vision of heaven is clouded. Steele's hymn "The Transforming Vision of God"[38] is based on Psalm 17:15, "As for me, I will behold thy face in righteousness: I shall be satisfied, when I awake, with thy likeness." Here the speaker delights in God's presence and anticipates the day when God Himself will appear, for then God shall be seen as He truly is.[39] The best of what humanity has to offer cannot compare to the pure righteousness and holiness of God.

> My God, the visits of thy face
>> Afford superior joy,

> And teach my longing mind
> The path of life to find;
> A path proud science never found
> In all her wide, unwearied round;
> A path by bold philosophy untry'd:
> Nor will I ask the twinkling eyes of night;
> The sacred Word alone directs my flight,
> Nor can I miss my way with this unerring guide.

38. Steele, *Poems on Subjects Chiefly Devotional & Miscellaneous Pieces*, Hymn 15, 50–52.

39. Aalders notes that the reference to the face of God symbolizes His "very near presence," for which the speaker here longs. Aalders, *To Express the Ineffable*, 167.

> To all the flatt'ring world can give,
>   Or mortal hopes employ.

In the above verse, the speaker's encounters with God are described as "visits." Although such encounters attest that God is surely the "superior joy," they nonetheless fail to endure. Depicted as "clouds and darkness," sin is the barrier to seeing God in all His glory. Rather than being satisfied with His presence, the sinful heart is prone to wander and be entertained by the world's lowly activities.

> But clouds and darkness intervene,
>   My brightest joys decline,
> And earth's gay trifles oft ensnare
>   This wand'ring heart of mine.

The speaker appeals to God to deliver her from sin. Only God has the power to transform her current depraved condition, which roams the world thirstily (yet unsatisfied). The speaker sees herself as a dying soul needing the "enliv'ning ray" of God.

> Lord, guide this wand'ring heart to thee:
>   Unsatisfy'd I stray:
> Break thro' the shades of sense and sin,
>   With thine enliv'ning ray.

Only by God's deliverance will her soul be "fit" for a greater purpose, a heavenly one.

> O let thy beams resplendent shine,
>   And ev'ry cloud remove;
> Transform my pow'rs, and fit my soul
>   For happier scenes above.

With the cloud removed, Christ Himself is the revelation. When the day comes, the speaker looks forward to bearing her Savior's likeness. It is the hope that she will one day shed her sullied clothing and put on His "divine array" that transforms her vision. In verses 5 to 8, the speaker marvels at the wonders that await her, wonders that will see neither disruption nor end.

There Jesus reigns! May I be cloath'd
　　With his divine array;
And when I close these eyes in death,
　　Awake to endless day:

To endless day! to perfect life!
　　To bliss without alloy!
Where not the least faint cloud shall rise,
　　To intercept the joy:

To view, unveil'd, thy radiant face,
　　Thou everlasting fair!
And, chang'd to spotless purity,
　　Thy glorious likeness wear:

To feast, with ever new delight,
　　On uncreated good;
And drink full satisfying draughts
　　Of pleasure's sacred flood.

The speaker's reflection on the future glory overwhelms her. To wake in the likeness of God—to relish in true goodness, in abundance never ending—is an elusive vision. If it were possible, the speaker wishes that her thoughts could remain on eternity, but sin is always an unwanted impediment. The hymn concludes with an appeal to God to strengthen her faith and hope so she might not be prevented from taking joy in reflecting on the future glory.

O bliss too high for mortal thought!
　　It awes, and yet inspires:
Fain would my soul, unfetter'd, rise
　　In more intense desires.

Lord, raise my faith, my hope, my heart,
　　To those transporting joys;
Then shall I scorn each little snare,
　　Which this vain world employs:

Then, though I sink in death's cold sleep,
　　I shall awake to bliss,

> And in the likeness of my God,
> Find endless happiness.

Steele's hymn "Longing for Immortality"[40] is based on 2 Corinthians 5:4, "For we that are in this tabernacle do groan, being burdened: not for that we would be unclothed, but clothed upon, that mortality might be swallowed up of life." While the previous hymn applies the imagery of light and darkness to convey the speaker's inability to see God as He truly is, this hymn compares the body to a house of clay, which prevents the speaker from seeing the "eternal mansion" that awaits her. In verses 1 to 3, the house of clay image (signifying human frailty and corruption) evokes the feeling of imprisonment, and hence the speaker's desire for liberty. Liberty in this case can only mean eternity with God since "sins, and griefs, and pains" occupy all of earthly living.

> Sad pris'ners in a house of clay,
> With sins, and griefs, and pains opprest,
> We groan the ling'ring hours away,
> And wish, and long to be releas'd.
>
> Nor is it liberty alone,
> Which prompts our restless ardent sighs;
> For immortality we groan,
> For robes and mansions in the skies.
>
> Eternal mansions! bright array!
> O blest exchange! transporting thought!
> Free from th' approaches of decay,
> Or the least shadow of a spot!

The feeling of imprisonment is expressed in more elaborate terms in verse 4, where mortality is seen to inflict not only the individual but also the world. Here Steele's metaphors shatter any mistaken belief that the present visible world reigns supreme: the

---

40. Steele, *Poems on Subjects Chiefly Devotional & Miscellaneous Pieces*, Hymn 56, 110–11.

grandness of the "wide extended empire" is witnessed as sinking
into the vast ocean of eternity.

> There shall mortality no more
> Its wide extended empire boast,
> Forgotten all its dreadful pow'r,
> In life's unbounded ocean lost.

Until then the speaker's vision remains obstructed. But the
depth of her longing invites commiseration—she is a prisoner, sigh-
ing, groaning, desperate for a "glimpse" of eternal light to shine into
her prison. It is this longing that brings forth the "dawn of immortality," allowing it to penetrate her prison walls.

> Bright world of bliss! O could I see
> One shining glimpse, one cheerful ray
> (Fair dawn of immortality!)
> Break through these tott 'ring walls of clay.

It is this longing that leads her to Jesus. Jesus grants her a glimpse
of the eternal home that is before her. Although she inhabits a house
of clay, when the time comes, it will collapse. While it imprisons, it
is only temporary.

> Jesus, in thy dear name I trust,
> My light, my life, my Saviour God;
> When this frail house dissolves in dust,
> O rise me to thy bright abode.

The Conscious Desire for the Divine

Steele's hymn "Longing after Unseen Pleasures"[41] focuses on themes
similar to those in the former hymns. The speaker desires to possess
an unhindered view of heaven and begrudges the many temptations
the world dangles before her eyes. The cost of giving in to the world
is serious: not only has the speaker foregone "immortal joys" but also
risks being a "stranger" to it. The hymn is based on 2 Corinthians

---

41. Steele, *Poems on Subjects Chiefly Devotional & Miscellaneous Pieces,*
Hymn 50, 103–4.

4:18, which is a significant verse since it appears in the frontispiece of one of Steele's publications: "While we look not at the things which are seen, but at the things which are not seen: for the things which are seen are temporal; but the things which are not seen are eternal."[42]

> How long shall earth's alluring toys
>> Detain our hearts and eyes;
> Regardless of immortal joys,
>> And strangers to the skies?

The speaker therefore reminds herself of the consequences of allowing earth's "toys" to grab the spotlight in her life. The toy metaphor, which calls attention to the toy's meager value and purpose (for diversion), is elaborated on in verses 2 and 3. Although it is true that the pleasures of earth have their bright days (the phrase "brightest day" is repeated in both verses), their fated end deprives them of their prospect to fully satisfy.[43] Ironically the speaker acknowledges

---

42. See Aalders, *To Express the Ineffable*, 88, where the verse is printed on the frontispiece of the second volume of Anne Steele's *Poems on Subjects Chiefly Devotional*. Here Aalders describes the illustration and its significance: "The frontispiece…shows a woman with a tongue of flame above her head, holding a telescope or 'glass.' She gestures toward another woman who gazes to heaven while leaning on an anchor, emblematic of the Christian hope of the cross…. Central to this frontispiece is the presence of light—flame, rays, and 'glass'—which bring intellectual and spiritual enlightenment as they focus the mind and heart on God." Aalders, *To Express the Ineffable*, 87.

43. In Steele's poem "On Children's Play," in *Poems on Subjects Chiefly Devotional & Miscellaneous Pieces*, 218–19, she compares the joys of adulthood with the toys of childhood and youth, the former possessing no more value than the latter. The excerpt below (verses 1 to 8) illustrates Steele's remarkable ability to balance playfulness of verse (which reflects the theme of the poem) with seriousness of message.

> Oft, when the child in wanton play
> Exerts his little pow'rs,
> And busy, trifling, toils away
> In sports the circling hours;

> We smile to see his infant mind
> So eager, so intent;

that she is aware of this reality: "With conscious sighs we own." Even the "smile" of the bright noonday is unable to supply real joy because of the apprehension that nighttime will soon arrive.

> These transient scenes will soon decay,
>   They fade upon the sight;
> And quickly will their brightest day
>   Be lost in endless night.
>
> Their brightest day, alas, how vain!
>   With conscious sighs we own;

> But growing years new follies find,
> As much on trifles bent.
>
> Youth has its toys, when pleasure's charms
> The fond pursuit invite:
> But pleasure mocks th' extended arms;
> Vain shadow of delight!
>
> What are the joys of riper age?
> By time is folly cur'd?
> No, trifles still the heart engage,
> And vanity matur'd.
>
> If glitt'ring riches tempt the eyes,
> An envy'd, valu'd store;
> Thus children shells and counters prize,
> And hoard and wish for more.
>
> Or if aspiring fame employs
> The eager, gazing train;
> The paper-kite of sportive boys
> Is not more light and vain.
>
> Unsatisfy'd, and tir'd at last,
> We must resign our breath,
> Life's empty cares and follies past,
> And ev'ning close in death.
>
> Thus children weary of their play,
> With fretfulness oppress'd,
> Throw all their little toys away,
> And gently sink to rest.

> While clouds of sorrow, care and pain,
>   O'ershade the smiling noon.

The tone of this hymn is more of solemn longing than eager expectation, and verses 4 and 5 show the speaker's desire to escape her dark world. She recognizes that her vision of heaven is limited, her human sense and reason possessing a "feeble ray." As much as she aspires to raise her thoughts to heaven, she cannot do it on her own, though she has tried ("in ever-blooming prospect rise"). In other words, not only has her reliance on earthly toys held her back in a dark world but also her attempt to rely on herself to see heaven.

> O could our thoughts and wishes fly,
>   Above these gloomy shades,
> To those bright worlds beyond the sky
>   Which sorrow ne'er invades.
>
> There joys unseen by mortal eyes
>   Or reason's feeble ray,
> In ever-blooming prospect rise,
>   Unconscious of decay.

Having painted such a dark world in the initial verses, it is no surprise that Steele presents a contrast in the final two verses of the hymn. The speaker is convinced that the slightest inspiration from God will be apt to inspire her to look upward. The world thereupon becomes supremely bright as the speaker witnesses a "light divine" and "hearts inflame." These images of brightness depict a vision that has finally been ignited with divine passion.

> Lord, send a beam of light divine,
>   To guide our upward aim;
> With one reviving touch of thine,
>   Our languid hearts inflame.

Faith once again is the means by which the speaker's vision is transported to heaven. The metaphor of "faith's sublimest wing" shows that the speaker has the hope at last of rising upward.

> Then shall on faith's sublimest wing
>> Our ardent wishes rise
> To those bright scenes, where pleasures spring
>> Immortal in the skies.

Steele's hymn "Aspiring towards Heaven"[44] paints a beautiful portrait of the mortal yearning to break free from the boundaries of earth so she can take flight into heaven.[45] Much like the earlier hymns, the first two verses of this hymn begin with the speaker's scorn for what the "vain world" has to offer.

> Vain world, be gone, nor vex my heart
>> With thy deluding wiles;
> Hence, empty promiser, depart
>> With all thy soothing smiles.

> Superior bliss invites my eyes,
>> Delight unmix'd with woe;
> Now let my nobler thoughts arise,
>> To joys unknown below.

The verses that follow employ imagery so vivid that they almost navigate the singer/reader's imagination. Consider verse 3, for instance, where the starry sky is depicted as the "pavement" of heaven:

> Yon starry plains, how bright they shine,
>> With radiant specks of light;
> Fair pavement of the courts divine,
>> That sparkles on the sight!

The imagery is reinforced by the speaker's expressed desire to draw closer to the stars, not because of what the stars themselves have to offer but because of what is just beyond them. While heaven might at first have felt like some faraway place, Steele skillfully creates a

44. Steele, *Poems on Subjects Chiefly Devotional & Miscellaneous Pieces*, Hymn 77, 138–39.

45. For a discussion of some of Steele's poems that compare the mortal mind to a bird, see Aalders, *To Express the Ineffable*, 140–41.

concrete spatial relationship that brings the speaker closer to where she aspires.

> 'Tis distance lessens ev'ry star;
>   Could I behold them nigh,
> Bright worlds of wonder would appear
>   To my astonish'd eye!

Depicting the starry sky as the floor of heaven, Steele makes it appear as though the speaker is so close to heaven she can almost touch it. In verses 5 and 6, Steele describes the anxiousness and thrill of the speaker in trying to succeed in her efforts. In verse 7, success seems close as the speaker can almost hear the singing of heaven's angels.

> Thus heav'nly joys attract my eyes,
>   My heart the lustre warms;
> But could I reach those upper skies,
>   How infinite their charms!
>
> Come, heav'n-born faith, and aid my flight,
>   And guide my rising thought,
> Till earth, still lessening to my sight,
>   Shall vanish, quite forgot.
>
> But when to reach those blissful plains
>   Her utmost ardour tries,
> And almost hears the charming strains
>   Of hymning angels rise.

In the subsequent verse, Steele sustains the flight imagery. When coming to the recurring theme of sin acting as a barrier to the speaker's goal, she uses the metaphor of mortality as being a "painful load," its weight preventing the speaker from flying free. The imagery of the starry sky is incorporated subtly here: the speaker does not simply descend to earth but into the night where the stars reside. This image therefore hints that the speaker had actually come close to heaven, for she has fallen to the stars below.

> Mortality, with painful load,
>   Forbids the raptur'd flight;
> In vain she means Heaven's bright abode,
>   And sinks to earth and night.

Once again the hymn concludes with an appeal to God for strength and inspiration. Faith is what will lend the speaker stronger wings.[46] With these wings, the speaker has hope that one day she will indeed take flight to higher plains.

> O let thy love, my God, my King,
>   My hope, my heart, inspire;
> And teach my faith with stronger wing
>   To rise, and warm desire.

> Oft let thy shining visits cheer
>   This dark abode of clay,
> Till I shall leave these fetters[47] here,
>   And rise to endless day.

The hymn ends with a picture of hope, of a creature on the verge of flying, though not just yet. Glimpses of God's love, however, reassure the speaker of the joy that is to come.

---

46. In Steele's poem "The Elevation," in *Poems on Subjects Chiefly Devotional & Miscellaneous Pieces*, 326, it is Christ's work on the cross that relieves the speaker from her load:

> From awful Calvary the flight begins;
>   For there the burthen'd mind
>   Divine relief can find;
> 'Tis there she drops her load of sins;
> Accursed load, which held her from the skies!
>   'Tis love, almighty love,
>   Which bids the load remove.

47. "Chains for the feet." Johnson, *Dictionary of the English Language*, 73.

The Welcoming Arms of Christ

Steele's two hymns "The Glorious Presence of Christ in Heaven"[48] and "The Happiness of the Saints Above"[49] will be examined in conjunction with each other as they are based on a common verse, John 17:24: "Father, I will that they also, whom thou hast given me, be with me where I am; that they may behold my glory, which thou hast given me: for thou lovedst me before the foundation of the world." The former hymn presents the perspective of Christ the King at His throne; the latter hymn presents the perspective of those standing in the presence of the King.

In "The Glorious Presence of Christ in Heaven," Christ is the central figure. The bright ray of heaven is Jesus Himself. In verse 2, the King is seen at his throne, all others bowing in worship of Him. The verse conveys the sense that the saints and angels have been waiting for this moment all along, and at last the moment is theirs—their worship finally unhindered and no aspect of heaven withheld from them.

> O for a sweet inspiring ray,
> To animate our feeble strains,
> From the bright realms of endless day,
> The blissful realms, where Jesus reigns!
>
> There low before his glorious throne
> Adoring saints and angels fall,
> And with delightful worship own
> His smile their bliss, their heav'n, their all.

The tone of the hymn is exultant and celebratory. Christ, the rightful King, is crowned. In verse 3, the vastness of the heavens is seen joining in Christ's victory. As the hymn progresses, the focus remains on Christ. In verse 4, Christ is described as smiling; *all* of heaven is gazing at and praising Him.

---

48. Steele, *Poems on Subjects Chiefly Devotional & Miscellaneous Pieces*, Hymn 93, 160–61.

49. Steele, *Poems on Subjects Chiefly Devotional & Miscellaneous Pieces*, Hymn 94, 161–62.

> Immortal glories crown his head,
> While tuneful hallelujahs rise,
> And love, and joy, and triumph spread
> Through all th' assemblies of the skies.
>
> He smiles, and seraphs tune their songs
> To boundless rapture while they gaze;
> Ten thousand thousand joyful tongues
> Resound his everlasting praise.

This long-awaited moment is expressed again in verse 5 with the phrase "at last." The stirring reality of John 17:24 is presented here—not only have God's children been anticipating this moment, but Christ Himself has been waiting for His children to join Him in His glory (the recurring image of Christ smiling is therefore fitting). This truth, then, that Christ in heaven is expecting the arrival of his "fav'rites," should produce in His children even greater faith.

> There all the fav'rites of the Lamb
> Shall join at last the heav'nly choir;
> O may the joy-inspiring theme
> Awake our faith and warm desire.

The hymn ends with an appeal to Jesus to have the Spirit confirm the truth in the hearts of His children concerning all that is to come, an allusion perhaps to John 16:14, "[The Spirit] shall glorify me: for he shall receive of mine, and shall shew it unto you."

> Dear Saviour, let thy spirit seal
> Our int'rest in that blissful place;
> Till death remove this mortal veil,
> And we behold thy lovely face.

Although the hymn depicts a vivid and intimate image of Christ at His throne, the speaker nonetheless recognizes that it is the Spirit who enables her to sustain this vision.

In "The Happiness of the Saints Above," the words of Jesus recorded in John 17:24 are a great comfort. Fully accepting His words should elicit hope in the promised glory.

> O could we read our int'rest here,
> Jesus, in these dear words of thine,
> A heav'n of pleasure would appear,
> A blissful view of joys divine.

At the same time, verses 2 and 3 address a sobering reality that confronts His children: Are they deserving of the glory that awaits them? The speaker turns to Jesus for reassurance. Only Christ can remove guilt and fear so that the glories of heaven can truly be enjoyed.

> Dear Saviour, let thy boundless grace
> Remove our guilt, our fears remove;
> Then shall our thoughts with rapture trace
> The radiant mansions of thy love.

> There shall our hearts no more complain,
> Nor sin prevail, nor grace decay;
> But perfect joy forever reign,
> One glorious, undeclining day.

Unlike the former hymn in which the vision of heaven seems so clear, this latter hymn bears the character of many of the others discussed so far in this chapter: heaven is not yet in plain view, but there remains hope that one day it will be. On that day, God's children will partake in Christ's glory. Sacred words that at present merely offer comfort will ultimately bring immeasurable joy.

> No darkness there shall cloud our sight;
> There now dejected, feeble eyes,
> Shall gaze, with infinite delight,
> On the full glories of the skies.

> There shall we see thy lovely face,
> And chang'd to purity divine,
> Partake the splendors of the place,
> And in thy glorious likeness shine.

> Yes, dearest Lord, to dwell with thee,
> Thy praise our endless, sweet employ,
> Must be immense felicity,
> A full infinitude of joy!

The hymn concludes with the same appeal as the former hymn, the desire for the Spirit to grant assurance to believers of all that is to come.

> O let thy spirit now impart,
> The kind assurance of thy love,
> With sealing pow'r to ev'ry heart,
> Sweet earnest of the joys above.

It is important to note that both these hymns are written in the third-person plural while many of the earlier hymns are written in the first-person singular. In the earlier hymns, the speaker is communicating her own reflections on what awaits her in glory; but when communicating her thoughts on the actual day of glory, she does not simply envision herself standing in that glory, but herself along with all the saints. This deliberate reference to the collective is consistent with the image appearing in the hymns discussed earlier—that is, the universal or heavenly choir.

Inspiration for Worship

Steele's hymn "The Joys of Heaven"[50] provides insight into how visions of the future glory ought to inspire worship, though the reality is that such visions for the time being remain inadequate. In verse 1, the speaker appeals to God to stir in her visions of heaven:

> Come, Lord, and warm each languid heart,
>   Inspire each lifeless tongue;
> And let the joys of heav'n impart
>   Their influence to our song.

Her passion ignited, the speaker experiences exhilaration and utter delight in her worship, as described in verse 2. She is able to survey heaven's grounds and meditate on its joys.

> Then to the shining seats of bliss
>   The wings of faith shall soar,

---

50. Steele, *Poems on Subjects Chiefly Devotional & Miscellaneous Pieces*, Hymn 16, 52–54.

> And all the charms of Paradise
> Our raptur'd thoughts explore.

In verses 6 and 7, it is Christ on His throne that is the greatest reason for worship since He has redeemed her from sin. The speaker sits before her Savior in "spotless purity," unashamed, forgiven. The "shining [seat]" that the speaker occupies in verse 2 is juxtaposed with the "dazzling bright" seat of Christ's throne in verse 7. The absolute brilliance of Christ's glory leads the speaker to respond with "ineffable delight"; that is, there is no satisfying, earthly way to express her worship.[51]

> The soul, from sin for ever free,
>   Shall mourn its pow'r no more;
> But cloath'd in spotless purity,
>   Redeeming love adore.

> There on a throne, (how dazzling bright!)
>   Th' exalted Saviour shines;
> And beams ineffable delight
>   On all the heav'nly minds.

Later, in verse 10, the speaker recognizes that even her present vision is not a complete representation of her Redeemer's glory, though she nonetheless persists in the vision:

> How will the wonders of his grace
>   In their full lustre shine?
> His wisdom, pow'r, and faithfulness,
>   All glorious! all divine!

---

51. This is a theme explored by Aalders. In fact, this very hymn concludes Aalders's hymn analysis as she highlights Steele's Christ-centered spirituality: "Now glorified, the Lamb inspires eternal worship in those whose powers of speech, and thus ability to praise, were once compromised by a persisting sinfulness. In Christ, God brought near, the Word breaks the silence, transfiguring human praise through the experience of divine love, and creating a way for the fulfillment of human longing—the promised presence of God and the eschatological perfection of praise." Aalders, *To Express the Ineffable*, 171.

Ineffability is again the focus in verse 12. The future glory is too remarkable for the mind to ponder—the speaker is overwhelmed and feels her worship is inadequate, "and all our notes are faint."

> But oh! their transports, oh! their songs,
>   What mortal thought can paint?
> Transcendent glory awes our tongues,
>   And all our notes are faint.

Yet despite the inadequacy of the speaker's vision and her inarticulacy of the glorious nature of her Savior, she is able to discover ways to inspire worship.

It is interesting to observe the way Steele consciously determines the psychic distance between the speaker and the future glory in her hymns. In some hymns the speaker is so close to heaven she can envision Christ on His throne; in other hymns the speaker is remote from it. Steele's hymn "The Promised Land"[52] is an example of the latter. The sense of remoteness is seen in words such as "far," "unknown" (verse 1), and "distant" (verse 2). While the speaker longs for future glory, she comes to grips with reality—it is a blessing even to imagine *half* the joys of heaven.

> Far from these narrow scenes of night
>   Unbounded glories rise,
> And realms of infinite delight,
>   Unknown to mortal eyes.
>
> Fair distant land!—could mortal eyes
>   But half its joys explore,
> How would our spirits long to rise,
>   And dwell on earth no more!

Even in the face of this limitation, the speaker considers concrete reasons that the future glory will be a place to anticipate. In verse 3, pain and sickness will be supplanted by health; in verse 4, war by peace; in verse 5, fleeting amusements by everlasting joys; in

---

52. Steele, *Poems on Subjects Chiefly Devotional & Miscellaneous Pieces*, Hymn 87, 153–55.

verse 6, rivalry and envy by harmony and love; and finally, in verse 7, sin by eternal bliss and holiness.

> There pain and sickness never come,
>   And grief no more complains;
> Health triumphs in immortal bloom,
>   And endless pleasure reigns!
>
> From discord free, and war's alarms,
>   And want, and pining care,
> Plenty and peace unite their charms,
>   And smile unchanging there.
>
> There rich varieties of joy
>   Continual feast the mind;
> Pleasures which fill, but never cloy,
>   Immortal and refin'd!
>
> No factious strife, no envy there,
>   The sons of peace molest,
> But harmony and love sincere
>   Fill every happy breast.
>
> No clouds those blissful regions know,
>   Forever bright and fair!
> For sin, the source of mortal woe,
>   Can never enter there.

While in many of Steele's hymns the sun's brightness is used as a point of comparison with God's glory, in the distant land described in this hymn, the sun merely possesses a "faint sickly ray" (verse 8). The sun's lack of brightness is a metaphor for the disparity between heaven and earth—this reality having been demonstrated in the previous verses. The source of light in this distant land is Christ Himself, which shines eternally, unlike sunlight that vanishes upon the arrival of night.

> There no alternate night is known,
>   Nor sun's faint sickly ray;
> But glory from the sacred throne
>   Spreads everlasting day.

"The Promised Land" is based on Isaiah 33:17, "Thine eyes shall see the king in his beauty: they shall behold the land that is very far off." Reinforcing the theme of this hymn, Steele is careful to maintain a distance between the speaker and the land she envisions; in fact, the King is not even named in this hymn (verse 9 below), reflecting the reality that the speaker's vision of the future glory remains veiled.

> The glorious monarch there displays
> His beams of wond'rous grace;
> His happy subjects sing his praise,
> And bow before his face.

In the final verses of the hymn, the speaker hopes that, having conjured up reasons to anticipate the future glory, she might be inspired to worship more fervently. The verb "fire" appears as the last word of the first line, giving it emphasis and an expectation of what follows, and highlighting the moment of inspiration when the speaker is able to envision what awaits her in heaven.

> O may the heav'nly prospect fire
> Our hearts with ardent love,
> Till wings of faith and strong desire
> Bear ev'ry thought above.
>
> Prepare us, Lord, by grace divine,
> For thy bright courts on high;
> Then bid our spirits rise and join
> The chorus of the sky.

Victory over Death

On an ordinary day, thoughts of the future glory may not come to mind, but it certainly seems natural when death is an immediate reality[53]—and evidently this was something Steele wrestled with:

---

53. This was a cutting reality for Steele. Throughout her life, Steele suffered losses that included the early death of her mother; her stepmother, Anne Cator Steele (1760); her sister-in-law, Mary Bullock Steele (1762); her nephew, Samuel Wakeford (1767); her half-sister, Mary Steele Wakeford (1772); and her

"In her letters and verse, she repeatedly deals with the topic of death—both the endured deaths of those she loved and the thought of her own impending death. Death was a very near threat which claimed those nearest and dearest to her."[54] In Steele's "A Funeral Hymn," mourners are reminded to look heavenward for comfort.

> While to the grave our friends are borne,
> Around their cold remains

---

father, William Steele, whose death had the biggest impact on her. In the preface to the 1780 edition of Steele's hymns, Caleb Evans wrote that "the death of her honoured father, to whom she was united by the strongest ties of affectionate duty and gratitude, gave such a shock to her feeble frame, that she never entirely recovered it though she survived him some years." Her poetic eulogy included these lines:

> Ah! now one tender, one endearing tie
> That held me down to earth, death has torn off,
> And with it rent my heart strings—bid me come,
> To thee my refuge; prostrate at thy feet,
> O bid me say, with faith and humble hope,
> Heal, gracious father, heal my bleeding heart!
> Thy healing hand alone can bring relief
> For woes like mine; can bring what most I want,
> An humble resignation to thy will.
> How hard the lesson! (yet it must be learn'd)
> With full consent to say, 'Thy will be done.'

See also Aalders, *To Express the Ineffable*, 107–9, and Broome, *Bruised Reed*, 200–201.

In her heartfelt poem "A Meditation on Death," in *Poems on Subjects Chiefly Devotional & Miscellaneous Pieces*, 202–3, Steele vividly describes the emotional state of a mourner grieving over the deceased:

> What silent sorrow
> Sits on each visage, while their streaming eyes
> And wringing hands confess their inward anguish!
> Who can describe th' unutterable woe
> Which fills their hearts, to see a father, brother,
> A friend, in whom their all of earthly bliss
> Was center'd, gasping on the verge of life?

54. Aalders, *To Express the Ineffable*, 111.

How all the tender passions mourn,
  And each fond heart complains!

But down to earth, alas, in vain
  We bend our weeping eyes;
Ah! let us leave these seats of pain,
  And upward learn to rise.

Hope cheerful smiles amid the gloom,
  And beams a healing ray,
And guides us from the darksome tomb,
  To realms of endless day.

Jesus, who left his blest abode,
  (Amazing grace!) to die,
Mark'd, when he rose, the shining road
  To his bright courts on high.

To those bright courts, when hope ascends,
  The tears forget to flow;
Hope views our absent happy friends,
  And calms the swelling woe.[55]

In Steele's hymn "At the Funeral of a Young Person,"[56] the abrupt death of a loved one provokes even deeper reflection—the speaker's own death.

When blooming youth is snatch'd away
  By death's resistless hand,

---

55. Steele, *Poems on Subjects Chiefly Devotional & Miscellaneous Pieces*, Hymn 35, vv. 1–5, 85.

56. Steele, *Poems on Subjects Chiefly Devotional & Miscellaneous Pieces*, Hymn 57, vv. 1–2, 111. The same idea is expressed in Steele's poem "A Reflection, Occasioned by the Death of a Neighbour," in *Poems on Subjects Chiefly Devotional & Miscellaneous Pieces*, 267:

In life's gay bloom she falls; yet I am spar'd!
But wherefore this indulgence? Gracious God,
By this new admonition, teach my heart
How precious are the swiftly-flying hours
Which I supinely waste!

Our hearts the mournful tribute pay,
    Which pity must demand.

While pity prompts the rising sigh,
    O may this truth, impress'd
With awful pow'r—I too must die—
    Sink deep in ev'ry breast.

Steele does not hesitate to call attention to the reality at hand as she focuses on the stark image of a "gaping tomb."[57] Even greater cause for concern is the fact that death preys on the unsuspecting at any moment, sometimes even sooner than we think, as Steele points out in verse 3.

Let this vain world engage no more;
    Behold the gaping tomb!
It bids us seize the present hour,
    To-morrow, death may come.

In the previous hymn, Steele's objective is to comfort mourners, yet in this one it is evangelistic. In verse 4, the somber scene of death is the reason for the anxious to turn to God. In effect, the fear wrought in "ev'ry heart" is God's voice speaking to lost souls and those who have yet to find comfort in Him when facing death.

The voice of this alarming scene
    May ev'ry heart obey,
Nor be the heavenly warning vain,
    Which calls to watch and pray.

In the conclusion of the hymn (verse 6), peace is found in knowing that only God—who offers salvation through faith in His

---

57. Steele draws on the same image in her poem "A Meditation on Death," in *Poems on Subjects Chiefly Devotional & Miscellaneous Pieces*, 201–2:

Behold the gaping tomb! it seems to speak,
With silent horror, to my shiv'ring heart;
Bids me survey my swift approaching doom,
And view the dark retreat which waits my coming.

Son—can rightly prepare the soul for death. The repetition in the first line of the verse below, "O let us fly, to Jesus fly," reflects the earnestness and exigency of Steele's plea.

> O let us fly, to Jesus fly,
>   Whose pow'rful arm can save;
> Then shall our hopes ascend on high,
>   And triumph o'er the grave.
>
> Great God, thy sov'reign grace impart,
>   With cleansing, healing pow'r;
> This only can prepare the heart
>   For death's surprizing hour.

Steele's hymn "Death and Heaven"[58] sheds light on why the soul is in need of God in order to come to terms with death. The first three verses of the hymn describe the speaker's wonderment over her attachment to the world and her reluctance to leave it when the world has repeatedly been exposed for its shortcomings. Verses 4 and 5 then portray the speaker's fear of death. Death in these verses is personified; he is the "dreaded foe" with a "frown [of] terror" that glares into the speaker's "frighted eyes." The alliteration of *f* sounds provides emphasis and dramatic effect in verses 4 and 5.[59]

---

58. Steele, *Poems on Subjects Chiefly Devotional & Miscellaneous Pieces*, Hymn 70, 128–30.

59. Death as a fearsome opponent is a prominent image in Steele's hymns and poems. Consider her poem "A Reflection, Occasioned by the Death of a Neighbor," in *Poems on Subjects Chiefly Devotional & Miscellaneous Pieces*, 267:

> —Death is abroad;
> Close at my side he twangs his deadly bow.

In her poem "A Meditation on Death," in *Poems on Subjects Chiefly Devotional & Miscellaneous Pieces*, 267, she writes,

> —Death onward comes
> With hasty step, though unperceiv'd and silent.
> Perhaps (alarming thought!) perhaps he aims
> E'en now the fatal blow that ends my life.

> Whene'er I look with frighted eyes
> On death's impenetrable shade,
> Alas! what gloomy horrors rise,
> And all my trembling frame invade!
>
> O death, frail nature's dreaded foe,
> Thy frown with terror fills my heart;
> How shall I bear the fatal blow,
> Which must my soul and body part?

The reason for the speaker's fear of death is revealed in verses 6 and 7: sin. The speaker knows she cannot pass through this life free of guilt and regret. Death is the "dreaded foe" because it can snatch away her life before she has been freed from these chains.

> 'Tis sin which arms his dreadful frown,
> This only points his deadly sting;
> My sins which throw this gloom around,
> And all these shocking terrors bring.

Thus the speaker expresses the one truth for which she seeks assurance—that her sins have been forgiven.

> O could I know my sins forgiv'n,
> Soon would these terrors disappear;
> Then should I see a glimpse of heav'n,
> And look on death without a fear.

Christ is the Savior because of His atoning blood. In verse 9, only Christ, who grants the certainty of forgiveness, can ease the speaker's "doubting soul."

> O let thy love's all-pow'rful ray
> With pleasing force, divine control,
> Arise, and chase these clouds away,
> And shine around my doubting soul.

With Christ by her side, death, along with sin, is the forfeiter. Steele paints a picture of the battle in verse 11:

> With cheerful heart I then shall sing,
> And triumph o'er my vanquish'd foe—
> O death, where is thy pointed sting?
> My Saviour wards the fatal blow.

Battle imagery is developed fully in Steele's hymn "Victory over Death through Christ."[60] Death is so intimidating that the speaker feels "unequal to the dreadful fight" (verse 1). But when the speaker considers what her defense will be, the answer is unquestionably Jesus. While the speaker's natural instinct gives her every reason to be fearful, she relies on faith in verse 4 to keep her from surrendering to the terrifying powers of death.

> Jesus, be thou my sure defence,
>   My guard forever near;
> And faith shall triumph over sense,
>   And never yield to fear.

Steele does not circumvent the reality that must be faced. The speaker is, in fact, forced to face her own mortality on the battlefield. The battle scene depicted in these verses is intense. Yet while death is about to claim her life, she resolutely proclaims, "The conquest must be mine." Though in the battle her body is slain, she commits her spirit to God in verses 6 and 7. In this way death has not won.

> O may I meet the dreadful hour,
>   With fortitude divine;
> Sustain'd by thy almighty pow'r,
>   The conquest must be mine.

> What though subdued this body lies,
>   Slain in the mortal strife,
> My spirit shall unconquer'd rise
>   To a diviner life.

The speaker utters a heartfelt prayer, and it is as if we are first-hand witnesses to the speaker's final breath as she asks God to

---

60. Steele, *Poems on Subjects Chiefly Devotional & Miscellaneous Pieces*, Hymn 85, 150.

receive her departing spirit. We can almost imagine her body collapsing to the ground in verse 7.

> Lord, I commit my soul to thee,
> Accept the sacred trust,
> Receive this nobler part of me,
> And watch my sleeping dust:

This verse ends with a colon, which syntactically symbolizes that the speaker's death on the battlefield is not the end.

The final verses of the hymn paint a grand picture of a victorious army in heaven, paying tribute to the ultimate conqueror. The hymn therefore effectively delivers the message of 1 Corinthians 15:57: "But thanks be to God, which giveth us the victory through our Lord Jesus Christ."

> Till that illustrious morning come,
> When all thy saints shall rise,
> And cloath'd in full, immortal bloom,
> Attend thee to the skies.
>
> When thy triumphant armies sing
> The honours of thy name,
> And heav'n's eternal arches ring,
> With glory to the Lamb:
>
> O let me join the raptur'd lays,
> And, with the blissful throng,
> Resound salvation, pow'r, and praise,
> In everlasting song.

Conclusion

The hymns examined in this chapter reveal how Steele conjured up visions of heavenly glory, even as an inhabitant of earth. She believed that an authentic faith meant that promises of the future glory ought to manifest in her thoughts and her worship—although sin was a barrier to her being able to fully embrace that glory. As a result, Steele needed to stir up desire for the divine. She willfully contemplated heavenly images depicted in Scripture and allowed herself to be comforted by them. Above all she pictured Jesus on His throne, joyfully awaiting her arrival. In this way, Steele's spiritual vision gave her the courage to face the end of her life, even amid incredible pain and suffering. Steele's spirituality, as seen in her hymns, therefore beautifully and compellingly exemplifies the riches that the Christian faith offers to the dying sinner.

My business, my important business
is to examine where my hope is fixed,
to seek earnestly to the God of grace
for the unerring influences of his Holy Spirit
to guide me in the way to heaven,
to strengthen my faith, my hope, and every grace,
to make me fit for that state of spotless purity,
and then receive me to himself.

CHAPTER FIVE

Anne Steele's Hymnody:
A Window into the Christian Journey

Many of Steele's hymns touch upon similar themes, though none are identical; one hymn may shed light on an aspect of a theme, and a different hymn on another. By bringing them together we come closer to forming a complete picture. Not every hymn is as effectively or articulately written. Certain hymns undoubtedly possess more memorable lyrics than others as great theological truths are conveyed through powerful imagery, compelling metaphors, deep emotion, and impressive concision.

The Heartfelt Honesty of Anne Steele

Hymns written in the first person add a highly personal note, especially when we are informed about the actual experiences of the hymn writer. Steele's honesty illuminates different points of the Christian journey, not simply the instances when we feel close to God or express our adoration of Him, but also instances when we feel confounded by or apprehensive of His inaccessibility. Steele does not attempt to disguise her very human perspective or experiences—that is, her doubts, her despair, her helplessness, her fears—but rather uses them to lay emphasis on her need of deliverance from them. Her approach in her hymns enables us to identify more easily with her experiences. None of us are free from moments of intense vulnerability and powerlessness, and to witness an individual such as Steele, as pious and earnest as she was in her spiritual journey, facing obstacles and setbacks like we do, offers great encouragement for our own spiritual journeys. As Aalders puts it: "For while there is certainly a need for spiritual confidence and declarative hymn-singing, Steele's hymns temper a tempting triumphalism, reminding us of our human finitude and allowing for those moments of spiritual uncertainty which regularly occur in our lives."[1]

The Unique Voice of Anne Steele in Light of Her Contemporaries

Steele's evolving into a significant hymn writer is also credited to the influence of other hymn writers, particularly Isaac Watts.[2] Both were of the Dissenting tradition and brought up in a Calvinistic context. On the one hand, both experienced trials of faith as a result of religious persecution and physical suffering; on the other hand, Steele did not receive the level of education that Watts had (though she came from a well-educated family).[3]

Steele's skillfulness as a hymn writer and follower of Watts can be seen in her ability to find the appropriate and best wording for a line or verse. Watts was highly conscious of words and their meaning, and while his hymnody is not "spectacularly metaphorical," he was extremely meticulous when it came to finding the ideal word without having it rob from the hymn's rhyme or rhythm.[4] Watts paid great attention to such details as "the way in which words, punctuation, stress, and rhythm become elements in the line, with the lines constituting the verse,"[5] as well as the manipulation of syllables, punctuation, and pause for effect, which facilitated the movement of lines and whole stanzas.[6] Poetic devices were used in such a way that the hymn singer/reader was not conscious of them. This deliberate aim toward simplicity of language and fluidity

---

1. Aalders, *To Express the Ineffable*, 177.
2. Broome provides a helpful survey of Watts's repertoire of hymns to demonstrate the model that Steele followed. See Broome, *Bruised Reed*, 159–75, for an examination of and comparison between the hymns of Watts and Steele.
3. Broome, *Bruised Reed*, 165.
4. Watson, *English Hymn*, 139.
5. Watson, *English Hymn*, 141.
6. Watson, *English Hymn*, 142.

served the ultimate purpose of making the Christian gospel accessible to the ordinary worshiper.[7]

A survey of Steele's hymns illustrates her efforts in emulating
her mentor.[8] Broome describes her work as "polished and carefully
worked out," although her skill was not equal to that of Watts. He

---

7. The following is an excerpt from Watts's preface to his *Hymns and
Spiritual Songs*. It underscores the importance of the hymn writer to focus on
content and to use sophistication and complexity of language only to serve the
former: "The whole Book is confined to three Sorts of Metre, and fitted to the
most common Tunes…. The Metaphors are generally sunk to the Level of vul-
gar Capacities. I have aimed at ease of Numbers and Smoothness of Sound, and
endeavoured to make the Sense plain and obvious; if the Verse appears so gentle
and flowing as to incure the Censure of Feebleness, I may honestly affirm, that
sometimes it cost me labour to make it so: Some of the Beauties of Poesy are
neglected, and some willfully defaced: I have thrown out the Lines that were too
sonorous, and given an Allay to the Verse, lest a more exalted Turn of Thought or
Language should darken or disturb the Devotion of the plainest Souls. But hence
it comes to pass, that I have been forced to lay aside many Hymns after they were
finished, and utterly exclude them from this Volume, because of the Bolder Figures of Speech that crowded themselves into the Verse, and a more unconfined
Variety of Number which I could not easily restrain." Isaac Watts, *Hymns and
Spiritual Songs* (London: J. Humphreys, for John Lawrence, 1707), iii–xiv.

John Wesley expresses the same conviction concerning language in the
preface of *A Collection of Hymns for the Use of the People Called Method-
ists*: "Here are no *cant* expressions, no words without meaning. Those who
impute this to us know not what they say. We talk common sense (whether
they understand it or not) both in verse and prose, and use no word but in a
fixed and determinate sense. Here are (allow me to say) both the purity, the
strength, and the elegance of the English language—and at the same time the
utmost simplicity and plainness, suited to every capacity…. What is infinitely
more moment than the spirit of Poetry is the spirit of Piety…. It is in this view
chiefly that I would recommend it to every truly pious reader: as a means of
raising or quickening the spirit of devotion, of confirming his faith, of enlivening his hope, and of kindling or increasing his love to God and man. When
poetry thus keeps its place, as the handmaid of piety, it shall attain, not a poor
perishable wreath, but a crown that fades not away." John Wesley, Charles
Wesley, and Frank Whaling, *John and Charles Wesley: Selected Writings and
Hymns* (Mahwah, N.J.: Paulist Press, 1981), 176–77.

8. See Watson, *English Hymn*, 191–93, 195, and 197 for a comparison
between Watts and Steele regarding their hymns.

observes, however, that Steele was equal in writing about matters that concerned the soul.[9] This was surely a result of the pain and suffering that she had to undergo throughout most of her life: "Her ill-health over many years had been sanctified to her."[10] As a result, Broome declares, "no one has excelled Anne Steele in her tender, memorable, sensitive expression of the heart feelings of a tempted, exercised, tried Christian."[11] The hardships that Steele had to face compelled her to search out the God in whom her faith rested in a way that depicted a very real picture of the Christian journey.

For Watts the joy derived from creation was central to his theology, a theme that has also been seen in Steele's hymns. Creation reveals the existence of God, His wonders, His power, His goodness; it makes known to the individual his or her standing before and obligation to God. At the same time, creation itself is not sufficient, for special revelation is necessary to lead an individual to Christ.[12] Watts also had to endure frequent bouts of illness. Just as Steele had expressed in her prose, Watts also knew he had to be deliberate in recalling the divine graces: "Amid all the violence of my distemper and the tiresome months of it I thank God I never lost sight of reason and religion though sometimes I had much ado to preserve the machine of animal nature in such order as regularly to exercise either the man or the Christian."[13] Watts also had a strong vision of the soul's journey to eternity. He saw the future state as the height of holiness and happiness. It was to be a day when the kingdom of God would reign and the soul would see Jesus.[14] Evident in Watts's hymns was his ability to make visible the heavenly glory, "like a landscape on a clear day…and it is this clarity which marks so many of Watts's finest hymns. They work because they are assured, and

9. Broome, *Bruised Reed*, 165.

10. Broome, *Bruised Reed*, 165.

11. Broome, *Bruised Reed*, 175.

12. Watson, *English Hymn*, 134–35.

13. David G. Fountain, *Isaac Watts Remembered 1674–1748* (Burlington, Ontario: Joshua Press, 1998), 65.

14. Watson, *English Hymn*, 136.

they are assured because they are clear."[15] While some of Steele's hymns demonstrate this clear vision of heavenly glory, oftentimes she differed from Watts because she simultaneously expressed the struggle of sustaining this vision.

The lyrics in Watts's hymns expressed clarity and confidence because he saw faith as a "matter of seeing clearly."[16] Arnold observes that Steele's approach in her hymns differed from that of Watts and Wesley precisely because she was uninhibited when it came to articulating the doubts and struggles of the Christian journey.[17] He argues that Steele's hymns remain meaningful and convictive today because they provide a "dimension of spiritual thought for the congregational hymn-singer/reader, a dimension which [is] perhaps somewhat more central and applicable to the day-to-day vicissitudes of Christian living."[18] Furthermore, he offers a thoughtful account for the content and nature of Steele's hymns, which made her a unique hymn writer in her own right:

---

15. Watson, *English Hymn*, 139.

16. Watson, *English Hymn*, 141.

17. Consider the comparison that Arnold makes between Watts and Wesley and Steele: "One is always mindful of Steele struggling to write, to praise—a task that the earlier writers took for granted and did not examine. While Watts magically draws back the curtain on God's creation, and Wesley has no trouble probing the feelings of the individual Christian's heart, Steele seems to be fully occupied in trying to put words onto the page, words that she knows can never adequately perform the function she wants them to perform. Perhaps because of this realization, her tone is remarkably unlike that found in Watts, Wesley, or any other contemporary or previous hymn-writer. For the first time, hymns appear which portray, and do not resolve, doubt and struggle, and which portray a writer acknowledging a form of defeat rather than celebrating a form of victory." Richard Arnold, "A 'Veil of Interposing Night': The Hymns of Anne Steele (1717–1778)," *Christian Scholar's Review* 18, no. 4 (June 1989): 379.

Aalders provides a sample comparison between Watts and Wesley and Steele, where she uses Watts's popular hymn, "When I Survey the Wondrous Cross" as a way of illustrating Wesley's and Steele's different adaptations of it. Wesley's version of this hymn demonstrates his "exuberant confidence" and "infectious enthusiasm," while Steele's version is "tender, introspective…self-chastising." See Aalders, *To Express the Ineffable*, 124–27.

18. Arnold, "A 'Veil of Interposing Night,'" 382.

Steele's hymns are less a finished ideal or vision and more a point of departure for questions and reflection—less a portrait and more an exploration. Paradoxically, by never quite seeming to *begin* as hymns, their main effect is to encourage a reader or singer to ask certain fundamental questions about his or her position in God's grand scheme, and about the possibilities of God's response to, and intervention in, the Christian's life and aspirations. By continually questioning and doubting as such, there is a greater possibility that the reader can gain a clearer and more sharply defined perception of his or her own faith, a faith which, subject to this continual exercise, can become more supple and less static, and needs to be more closely attended to and less taken for granted and routinely celebrated. The sense of immediacy and heartfelt pleading—even desperation—in Steele's hymns tends to encourage an ongoing and variegated *process* of faith rather than the continual re-affirmation of a finished *state of faith*.[19]

Broome writes, "Anne knew the reality of the 'trial of faith.' Her hymns are pervaded from beginning to end with a desire for assurance. Prayer was for her the breath of her life. To walk in the light of God's countenance was her one desire."[20] Her journey of faith, he upholds, exemplified the words of Paul in Philippians 3:12: "Not that I have already obtained this or am already perfect, but I press on to make it my own, because Christ Jesus has made me his own."[21] Karen Smith notes that "while assurance was not the essence of faith, those who diligently searched, acquired knowledge of it."[22] In fact, Steele's father had preached on this very subject, specifying three aspects of faith, which Smith summarizes in her essay:

Credence, reliance, and assurance. Faith of credence and reliance, according to him, meant that one gave credit to the truth

19. Arnold, "A 'Veil of Interposing Night,'" 387.

20. Broome, *Bruised Reed*, 166.

21. Broome, *Bruised Reed*, 166.

22. Smith, "Covenant Life of Some Eighteenth-Century Calvinistic Baptists," 173. Smith's essay studies how an individual's faith was cultivated and shared in the context of the church, in particular Steele's church.

of what is revealed in Scripture and relied on Christ for salvation. Faith of assurance, on the other hand, meant that one had a "well grounded and full persuasion" of an interest in Christ. While the first two were by far the most important, he nevertheless urged listeners to strive to attain the latter. All believers, he wrote, "Must labor to get our evidences clear for heaven, we should not only labor to be sure we have faith of reliance and dependence on Christ, but indever [*sic*] to improve it to the faith of assurance."[23]

Perhaps the nature of Steele's faith can be better understood in the context of her father's sermon—that is, Steele was laboring for a "faith of assurance," perpetually striving for a more real and personal union with God. The active nature of Steele's faith, as Aalders sees it, is best seen in her endeavors as a writer, "for it was precisely in the act of writing that Steele attempted to work out her faith as well as the implications of those beliefs."[24] By "searching for words, a conscious labour to articulate what eluded expression," Steele was trying to "understand God," demonstrating that her faith was one of "persistent hopefulness" and "intense longing."[25]

---

23. William Steele, sermon on Psalm 39:5 (n.d.), Angus Library, Regent's Park College, Oxford; quoted in Smith, "Covenant Life of Some Eighteenth-Century Calvinistic Baptists," 173–74.

Wallace explains the topic of assurance in the context of Calvinism: "English Calvinist authors probed the nature of Christian living with an insistence, thoroughness, and degree of introspection that was to make them pacesetters in the Reformed world in this regard.... This literature concerned itself with moral duties, the morphology of the Christian life, and above all with the question of assurance: what were the evidences that one was in a state of grace and among the elect? Books and sermons that encouraged self-examination and analyzed cases of conscience played a key role in this development." Wallace, "English Calvinism in a New Era," 18.

24. Aalders, *To Express the Ineffable*, 148.

25. Aalders, *To Express the Ineffable*, 148. Even the order in which the hymns are arranged in Steele's manuscript, Aalders observes, "reflects her desire to set her spiritual anxieties in the context of Christian hope." Aalders, *To Express the Ineffable*, 162.

Learning from Anne Steele's Faith

What can be said of Steele's faith is that, in essence, she refused to be an idle believer. Instead of blindly or passively accepting the circumstances of her life, she was determined to understand those circumstances in the context of her relationship with God. She worked out her faith in her writing, in the solitude of her country-side home. Being a resident of the small village of Broughton for most of her years, she did not write from an external life full of complex and alien struggles others were exposed to when away from the comforts of home. Rather she wrote from an internal life that, though more quotidian, was no less consequential in shaping her spirituality.[26] Steele boldly wrestled with the issues of her faith and at the same time was assured of their resolutions (her hope anchored in Christ). She took seriously the discipline of divine meditation: it was through examining the motivations of her heart and reflecting on the weaknesses of her faith that she sought to strengthen her faith, as she writes in one poem:

> Kind Solitude, I love thy friendly shade;
> Reflection hither bring her needful aid.
> 'Tis here I trace past thoughts and errors o'er,
> And learn to know my weakness, and deplore.
> Ah! Would the serious, sad compunction last,
> And teach to mend the future by the past.[27]

Later in the poem she states her life's goal, confessing how little she knew of it but spurred nonetheless in its pursuit.

---

26. John Sheppard, in his preface to the 1863 publication of Steele's works, wrote: "She founded no church, built no chapels, went on no foreign mission. She only wrote a few of the sweetest hymns; but in thus using the poetical talent, which she recognised as divine, she did that which exceeds in importance and value the works of many who have filled more conspicuous places in the history of the church and of the world."

27. Steele, "Retirement and Meditation," *Poems on Subjects Chiefly Devotional & Miscellaneous Pieces*, 289.

All my celestial hopes on God depend;
His smile my life, his favour is my end.
How little do I know, or love his name!
And yet to spirits of immortal frame,
Knowledge is food, and love the vital flame.[28]

Then she poses the question, "How shall I know and love him?"[29] And from her writings, witnessing the spiritual journey on which she had embarked, we see the process by which she comes to answer this vital question, a process that ultimately led to an intensely more intimate and reverential view of her Savior. As a result, 250 years or so later, even though few of Steele's hymns remain in congregational use, many of them are considered invaluable for devotional use.[30]

Hymns have been said to guide us toward spiritual maturity because they reveal how we can arrive at a true knowledge of God. When we come to love the truth, we come to understand it, and it becomes all that we are and all that we do.[31] It has been seen that Steele's hymns and the life she led reflect this journey. Her exploration of God in her hymns involved honest questions, heartfelt prayers, examinations of Scripture, narratives brought to life, and emotional outpourings of the heart. Against the backdrop of life's mundanity, struggle, doubt, suffering, and transient joys, Steele held onto her faith because of her spiritual vision. She loved God, trusted Him, surrendered to Him, knew Him. She saw that everything in her life belonged to God, including her gift of writing (her penname, Theodosia, means "gift of God"). She strongly believed

---

28. Steele, "Retirement and Meditation," *Poems on Subjects Chiefly Devotional & Miscellaneous Pieces*, 290.

29. Steele, "Retirement and Meditation," *Poems on Subjects Chiefly Devotional & Miscellaneous Pieces*, 291.

30. Most modern hymnbooks include the following hymns by Anne Steele (based on the hymns' first lines): "Father of mercies, in thy Word," "When sins and fears prevailing rise," and "And did the Holy and the Just." Broome, *Bruised Reed*, 152.

31. Jeffrey P. Greenman and George R. Sumner, *Unwearied Praises: Exploring Christian Faith through Classic Hymns* (Toronto: Clements Publishing, 2004), 184–85.

that the origin of her inspiration and creativity was her faith, and thus knew it was her duty to offer her poetic talents for the purpose of glorifying her Creator.[32] And so we are able to reap the fruits of her personal journey in seeking God and celebrate with her when she at last discovers Him—her assurance becoming our assurance, and her liberation, ours.

---

32. Replying to a letter from an unnamed woman, Steele wrote that "sacred Poesy" is best used "in the service of Religion." Anne Steele (August 8, 1761), STE 3/13 (vii), Angus Library, Regent's Park College, Oxford; quoted in Aalders, *To Express the Ineffable*, 35.

Selected Bibliography

Aalders, Cynthia Y. *To Express the Ineffable: The Hymns and Spirituality of Anne Steele*. Studies in Baptist History and Thought, vol. 40. Milton Keynes, U.K.: Paternoster, 2008.

"Anne Steele's 'Psalm 13': A Hymn to Be Mined." *Perspectives in Religious Studies* 25, no. 1 (1998): 127–28.

Arnold, Richard. "A 'Veil of Interposing Night': The Hymns of Anne Steele (1717–1778)." *Christian Scholar's Review* 18, no. 4 (June 1989): 371–87.

Bath, Michael, and Tom Furniss. "Hearing Voices in Poetic Texts." In *Reading Poetry: An Introduction*, 159–61. Hertfordshire: Prentice Hall/Harvester Wheatsheaf, 1996.

Benson, Louis. *The English Hymn, Its Development and Use in Worship*. New York: Hodder and Stoughton, 1915.

Brodey, Inger S. B. "On Pre-Romanticism or Sensibility: Defining Ambivalences." In *A Companion to European Romanticism*, 10–26. Edited by Michael Ferber. Malden, Mass.: Blackwell Publishing, 2005.

Broome, J. R. *A Bruised Reed: The Life and Times of Anne Steele*. Harpenden, U.K.: Gospel Standard Trust Publications, 2007.

Burrage, Henry S. *Baptist Hymn Writers and Their Hymns*. Portland, Maine: Brown Thurston and Company, 1888.

Calhoun, David. "The Great Divide: Enlightenment and Romanticism." Lecture given at Covenant Theological Seminary, St. Louis, Mo., Spring 2006. http://worldwidefreeresources.com/upload/CH320_T_22.pdf.

Davie, Donald. *The Eighteenth-Century Hymn in England.* Cambridge Studies in Eighteenth-Century English Literature and Thought. New York: Cambridge University Press, 1993.

Dixon, Michael F., and Hugh F. Steele-Smith. "Anne Steele's Health: A Modern Diagnosis." *Baptist Quarterly* 32 (July 1988): 351–56.

Dobson, Mary J. *Contours of Death and Disease in Early Modern England.* Cambridge Studies in Population, Economy and Society in Past Time, vol. 29. New York: Cambridge University Press, 1997.

Dudley-Smith, Timothy. "The Poet as Hymn Writer." In *The Christian Imagination*, 387–96. Edited by Leland Ryken. Colorado Springs: WaterBrook, 2002.

Fountain, David G. *Isaac Watts Remembered 1674–1748.* 3rd ed. Burlington, Ontario: Joshua Press, 1998.

Gill, John. *A Body of Practical Divinity.* The Baptist Faith Series, vol. 2. Paris, Ark.: The Baptist Standard Bearer, 2001.

———. *Complete Body of Practical and Doctrinal Divinity.* Edited by William Staughton. Philadelphia: Delaplaine and Hellings, 1810.

———. *The Dissenters' Reasons for Separating from the Church of England.* 4th ed. London, 1760.

Greenman, Jeffrey P., and George R. Sumner. *Unwearied Praises: Exploring Christian Faith through Classic Hymns.* Toronto: Clements Publishing, 2004.

Grudem, Wayne. *Systematic Theology: An Introduction to Biblical Doctrine.* Leicester, U.K.: InterVarsity, 1994.

Haykin, Michael A. G. "Benjamin Beddome and Anne Steele." In *The Christian Lover: The Sweetness of Love and Marriage in the Letters of Believers*, 31–35. Lake Mary, Fla.: Reformation Trust, 2009.

Hindmarsh, D. Bruce. "Retrieval and Renewal: A Model for Evangelical Spiritual Vitality." In *J. I. Packer and the Evangelical Future: The Impact of His Life and Thought*, 111. Edited by Timothy George. Grand Rapids: Baker Academic, 2009.

James, Sharon. *In Trouble and in Joy: Four Women Who Lived for God.* Darlington, U.K.: Evangelical Press, 2003.

Johnson, Samuel. *Dictionary of the English Language.* London: T. Noble, 1819.

Lind, James. "An Essay on Diseases Incidental to Europeans in Hot Climates. With the Method of Preventing Their Fatal Consequences." 3rd ed. London: T. Becket, 1777.

Lovelace, Austin C. *The Anatomy of Hymnody.* Chicago: G.I.A. Publications, 1965.

Manley, Ken R. "'Sing Side by Side': John Rippon and Baptist Hymnody." In *Pilgrim Pathways: Essays in Baptist History in Honour of B. R. White*, 127–63. Edited by William H. Brackney, Paul S. Fiddes, and John H. Y. Briggs. Macon, Ga.: Mercer University Press, 1999.

Noll, Mark, A. "We Are What We Sing: Our Classic Hymns Reveal Evangelicalism at Its Best." *Christianity Today* 43 (July 1999): 37–41.

Patterson, Lee. "Literary History." In *Critical Terms for Literary Study*, 250–62. Edited by Frank Lentricchia and Thomas McLaughlin. Chicago: University of Chicago Press, 1995.

Porter, Roy. "What Is Disease?" In *The Cambridge History of Medicine*, 95. Edited by Roy Porter. New York: Cambridge University Press, 2006.

Reardon, Bernard M. G. *Religion in the Age of Romanticism: Studies in Early Nineteenth-Century Thought.* New York: Cambridge University Press, 1985.

Reeves, Jeremiah Bascom. *Hymn as Literature.* New York: Century Company, 1924.

Reeves, Marjorie. *Pursuing the Muses: Female Education and Nonconformist Culture, 1700–1900.* London: Leicester University Press, 1997.

———. "Jane Attwater's Diaries." In *Pilgrim Pathways: Essays in Baptist History in Honour of B. R. White*, 207–22. Edited by William H. Brackney, Paul S. Fiddes, and John H. Y. Briggs. Macon, Ga.: Mercer University Press, 1999.

———. *Sheep Bell and Ploughshare: The Story of Two Village Families.* Bradford-on-Avon, U.K.: Moonraker Press, 1978.

Reymond, Robert L. *A New Systematic Theology of the Christian Faith.* 2nd ed. Nashville: Thomas Nelson, 1998.

Shaw, Jane. "Introduction: Why 'Culture and the Nonconformist Tradition'?" In *Culture and the Nonconformist Tradition*, 1–6. Edited by Jane Shaw and Alan Kreider. Cardiff: University of Wales Press, 1999.

Smith, Karen. "The Covenant Life of Some Eighteenth-Century Calvinistic Baptists in Hampshire and Wiltshire." In *Pilgrim Pathways: Essays in Baptist History in Honour of B. R. White*, 165–83. Edited by William H. Brackney, Paul S. Fiddes, and John H. Y. Briggs. Macon, Ga.: Mercer University Press, 1999.

Steele, Anne. *Hymns by Anne Steele*. Preface by J. R. Broome. London: Gospel Standard Baptist Trust, 1967.

———. *Hymns, Psalms and Poems, by Anne Steele*, with *Memoir by John Sheppard*. London: Daniel Sedgwick, 1863.

———. *Miscellaneous Pieces, in Verse and Prose, by Theodosia*. Bristol, U.K.: W. Pine, 1780.

———. *The Works of Mrs. Anne Steele: Complete in Two Volumes. Comprehending Poems on Subjects Chiefly Devotional: and Miscellaneous Pieces in Prose and Verse: Heretofore Published under the Title of Theodosia*. Boston: Munroe, Francis and Parker, 1808.

Wallace, Dewey D. "English Calvinism in a New Era." In *Shapers of English Calvinism, 1660–1714: Variety, Persistence, and Transformation*, 9–50. New York: Oxford University Press, 2011.

Watson, J. R. *The English Hymn: A Critical and Historical Study*. New York: Oxford University Press, 1997.

Watson, J. R. and Nancy Cho. "Anne Steele's Drowned Fiancé." *British Journal for Eighteenth-Century Studies* 28 (2005): 117–21.

Watts, Isaac. *Hymns and Spiritual Songs*. London: J. Humphreys, for John Lawrence, 1707.

Wesley, John, Charles Wesley, and Frank Whaling. *John and Charles Wesley: Selected Writings and Hymns*. Mahwah, N.J.: Paulist Press, 1981.